UNITED STATES OF AMERICA
DEPARTMENT OF STATE

The
James Earl Ray
Extradition File

PAPERS SUBMITTED TO GREAT BRITAIN
FOR THE EXTRADITION OF
JAMES EARL RAY
TO FACE TRIAL FOR THE MURDER OF
MARTIN LUTHER KING, JR.

LEMMA PUBLISHING CORPORATION
NEW YORK · 1971

THE JAMES EARL RAY EXTRADITION FILE

A Lemma Publishing Corporation Original Publication

Publication of this volume was not in any way
sponsored or supported by any governmental agency

Published by
Lemma Publishing Corporation
509 Fifth Avenue
New York, N. Y. 10017

Printed in U.S.A.

Publisher's Foreword

On the strength of the documents included in this volume, London's Chief Metropolitan Magistrate ruled that there was sufficient cause for the extradition of James Earl Ray from Great Britain to the United States to face trial for the murder of Martin Luther King, Jr., shot down on a Memphis motel balcony on April 4, 1968.

Submitted by the United States State Department to the British Home Office shortly after Ray's arrest in London on June 8, 1968, these papers were intended to establish Ray's identity, and to show that he had been accused in the United States of an extraditable crime, and that there was sufficient evidence to bring him to trial. They include depositions of F.B.I. ballistics, fingerprint, and handwriting experts; the official report of the autopsy performed on the body of Martin Luther King, Jr.; an official survey of the murder site; as well as affidavits from Memphis law-enforcement officers and from several key witnesses in the case, including the salesman who claims to have sold the alleged murder weapon to Ray, and a tenant of the rooming house from which the murder was purportedly committed.

Since Ray pleaded guilty to murder in the first degree at the opening of his trial on March 10, 1969, and no testimony was heard, the documents included in this volume constitute the most complete file of evidence against him published to date.

The material presented in this volume was transcribed verbatim from a machine copy of the original obtained from the United States Department of Justice. Since many of the original documents were gathered piecemeal, it was often found expedient to improve the order of presentation by rearranging their sequence in the process of transcription. In the original file, each document is accompanied by a long chain of certifications. While several of these certifications have been retained in order to preserve the flavor of the original document, many were found superfluous and repetitious, and were dropped. Had all certifications been retained, this volume would have grown to nearly twice its present size.

Contents

vi

vii

REQUEST FOR EXTRADITION

AMERICAN EMBASSY
London, June 12, 1968

1. The Ambassador of the United States of America at London presents his compliments to Her Majesty's Principal Secretary for Foreign Affairs and has the honor, on instructions of the Department of State, to request the extradition to the United States in accordance with the Extradition Treaty between the United States of America and Great Britain signed at London on December 22, 1931, of James Earl Ray, alias, Eric Starvo Galt, alias John Willard, alias Harvey Lowmeyer, alias Harvey Lowmyer, alias Ramon George Sneyd, alias Ramon George Sneya, alias W. C. Herron, alias James McBride, alias James O'Conner, alias James Walton, alias James Walyon, alias Paul Bridgman, alias "Jim," presently in custody in the United Kingdom under the name of Ramon George Sneyd for the crimes of murder and robbery with violence. Mr. Ray is presently under indictment in Shelby County in the State of Tennessee for murder in the first degree. This crime is covered by paragraph 1 of Article 3 of the Extradition Treaty between the United States of America and Great Britain. Mr. Ray has also been convicted of the crime of robbery, first degree by means of a dangerous and deadly weapon on December 17, 1959 in the city of St. Louis, State of Missouri, and sentenced on February 19, 1960 to be confined for a period of 20 years. He escaped from the Missouri State penitentiary on April 23, 1967, leaving an unexpired term with legal expiration of March

1

16, 1980. This crime is covered by paragraph 16 of Article 3 of the Extradition Treaty. Both the State of Tennessee and the State of Missouri have requested his extradition. Authenticated documents covering the aforementioned indictment and conviction are attached.

2. The Government of the United States of America is prepared to designate agents to receive Mr. Ray alias Eric Starvo Galt, alias John Willard, alias Harvey Lowmeyer, alias Harvey Lowmyer, alias Ramon George Sneyd, alias Ramon George Sneya, alias W. C. Herron, alias James McBride, alias James O'Conner, alias James Walton, alias James Walyon, alias Paul Bridgman, alias "Jim," in the United Kingdom and convey him to the United States at the proper time. Therefore, the Ambassador would be grateful if Her Majesty's Government would inform him when the agent or agents should come to this country to receive the said James Earl Ray, alias Ramon George Sneyd.

3. The law firm of Rowe and Maw, Stafford House, Strand, London, W.C. 2, has been authorized to represent the United States of America on the requisitions of the State of Tennessee and the State of Missouri in this matter.

Enclosures: Requisitions with attachments.

CERTIFICATION

GREAT BRITAIN AND NORTHERN IRELAND
LONDON, ENGLAND
EMBASSY OF THE UNITED STATES OF AMERICA

June 12, 1968

I, Wayne W. Fisher, Consul General of the United States of America at London, England, duly commissioned and qualified, do hereby certify that the annexed document is under the seal of the Department of State of the United States of America.

[Signed] Wayne W. Fisher
Consul General of the United States
of America at London, England.

DEPARTMENT OF STATE

all to whom these presents shall come, Greeting:

I Certify *That the document hereunto annexed is under the Seal of the State of* ....

.... *TENNESSEE* ....

In testimony whereof, I, ...*DEAN RUSK*, ...

Secretary of State, have hereunto caused the seal of the Department of State to be affixed and my name subscribed by the Authentication Officer of the said Department, at the city of Washington, in the District of Columbia, this ....*eleventh* ....

day of ....*June* ...., *19* ..*68* .

Secretary of State.

By ....

Authentication Officer, Department of State.

4

APPLICATION FOR REQUISITION
FOR INTERNATIONAL EXTRADITION

TO: THE HONORABLE DEAN RUSK, SECRE-
TARY OF STATE OF THE UNITED STATES
OF AMERICA

FROM: BUFORD ELLINGTON, GOVERNOR OF THE
STATE OF TENNESSEE

IN RE: STATE OF TENNESSEE VS JAMES EARL
RAY, alias ERIC STARVO GALT, alias JOHN
WILLARD, alias HARVEY LOWMEYER, alias
HARVEY LOWMYER, alias RAMON GEORGE
SNEYD

The applicant, the Governor of the State of Tennessee,
Buford Ellington, would state to the Secretary of State
that the offense of Murder has been committed within the
jurisdiction of the State of Tennessee, in the County of
Shelby, and that the person charged with this offense,
James Earl Ray, alias Eric Starvo Galt, alias John Willard,
alias Harvey Lowmeyer, alias Harvey Lowmyer, alias
Ramon George Sneyd, has been found in the Dominions of
the United Kingdom and is in custody in the city of
London, England. The applicant would state that this
fugitive was present in the State of Tennessee, in the
County of Shelby, at the time that the offense, with which
he is charged, was committed, and that, thereafter, he fled
from the State of Tennessee and the United States of
America. The applicant would state that he has received no

5

information that the fugitive would waive extradition.

The applicant would propose, for designation by the President of the United States, to receive and convey the prisoner to the United States and to the State of Tennessee, the county of Shelby, and the city of Memphis, the following:

_____

_____

_____

The applicant would state that this application is made, solely, for the purpose of bringing about the trial and punishment of the fugitive, and not for any private purpose, and that if the application is granted, the criminal proceedings will not be used for any private purpose.

Transmitted, herewith, to the Secretary of State, and by reference made a part of this application, is the attached sworn and certified Petition of the District Attorney General for the County of Shelby, the State of Tennessee; also transmitted, herewith, to the Secretary of State, and, by reference, made a part of this application, are the attached Certified copies of the Original Indictment, No. 16645, returned in the Criminal Court of Shelby County, Tennessee, at Memphis, Tennessee, on May 7th, 1968, and the Capias (Warrant of Arrest) No. 16646, issued in the Criminal Court of Shelby County, State of Tennessee, at Memphis, on May 7th, 1968.

Also transmitted, herewith, to the Secretary of State, and, by reference made a part of this application, are the attached copies of evidence, certified in due form, to wit,

Affidavit of Dr. J. T. Francisco
Affidavit of Robert V. Wenzler
Affidavit of Guy Warren Canipe, Sr.
Affidavit of Inspector N. E. Zachary
Affidavit of Captain R. L. Williams
Affidavit of Cordra York, Sr.
Affidavit of Lieutenant James D. Hamby

And certified copies thereof;

And Affidavit of Robert G. Jensen, Special Agent in Charge, Federal Bureau of Investigation, and certified copies thereof.

The applicant, Buford Ellington, hereby certifies that Joe C. Carr, Secretary of the State of Tennessee, whose true and genuine signature appears to the annexed certificates, with respect of the certifications of the attached copies of (1) The Death Certificate; (2) The Autopsy Report (Protocol) and (3) The Law of the State of Tennessee in respect to Murder, referred to above, as copies of evidence, is, and was, at the time of signing the same, certificates, the duly elected, qualified and commissioned Secretary of State of the State of Tennessee, and that his official acts, as such, are entitled to full faith and credit.

Further, the applicant, Buford Ellington, hereby certifies that Perry H. Sellers, Judge of Criminal Court, Division One, Shelby County, Memphis, Tennessee, whose true and genuine signature appears to the annexed certificates, with respect of the certification of the copies of the (1) Indictment in this case, (2) Capias (Warrant of Arrest) in this case, and, (3) Affidavits of: Dr. J. T. Francisco, Robert V. Wenzler, Guy Warren Canipe, Sr., Inspector N. E. Zachary, Captain R. L. Williams, Cordra York, Sr., Robert G. Jensen, and Lieutenant James D. Hamby, referred to above as the Indictment, Capias and Copies of Evidence, is, and, was at the time of signing the same certificates, the duly elected, qualified and commissioned Judge of the Criminal Court of Shelby County, Tennessee, and that his official acts, as such, are entitled to full faith and credit.

The applicant requests that the President of the United States issue a Requisition for the International Extradition of James Earl Ray, alias Eric Starvo Galt, alias John Willard, alias Harvey Lowmeyer, alias Harvey Lowmyer, alias Ramon George Sneyd, from the Dominions of the United Kingdom to the United States of America and to the State of Tennessee, the County of Shelby, in conformity with the treaty existing between the United Kingdom and the United States of America, which was signed on December 27, 1931, and which entered into force on June 24th, 1935. This treaty is embodied in 47 Stat. 2122 (1931).

In testimony whereof, I have hereunto set my hand and caused the Great Seal of the State of Tennessee to be affixed at the State Capitol in Nashville, Tennessee, on this the 11th day of June A.D. 1968.

[Signed] Buford Ellington
Governor of the State of Tennessee

PETITION FOR APPLICATION
FOR REQUISITION
IN INTERNATIONAL EXTRADITION

IN RE:
STATE OF TENNESSEE
VS.
JAMES EARL RAY, ALIAS ERIC STARVO GALT,
ALIAS JOHN WILLARD, ALIAS HARVEY LOW-
MEYER, ALIAS HARVEY LOWMYER, ALIAS RAMON
GEORGE SNEYD

TO HIS EXCELLENCY
THE HONORABLE BUFORD ELLINGTON
GOVERNOR OF THE STATE OF TENNESSEE

Your Petitioner, Phil M. Canale, Jr., would respectfully
present and show to Your Excellency, that:

I

Petitioner is the duly elected, qualified, commissioned and
serving District Attorney General for the Fifteenth Judicial
Circuit of the State of Tennessee, comprising the County
of Shelby, and that he is a resident citizen of Memphis,
Shelby County, Tennessee;

II

That one James Earl Ray, alias Eric Starvo Galt, alias John
Willard, alias Harvey Lowmeyer, alias Harvey Lowmyer,

alias Ramon George Sneyd, stands charged with the offense of Murder, as evidenced by the accompanied certified copies of an Indictment and a Capias;

III

That the Indictment, in this cause, was returned a True Bill by the Grand Jury of Shelby County, Tennessee, under date of May 7, 1968, and bears Criminal Court Docket No. 16645;

That the Capias, in this cause, was issued by J. A. Blackwell, Clerk of the Criminal Court of Shelby County, Tennessee, under date of May 7, 1968, and bears Criminal Court Docket No. 16645;

That the aforesaid two documents, consisting of Certified Copy of Indictment and Certified Copy of Capias, both documents having been certified, are hereto attached and herein made a part of this Petition for Requisition;

IV

That the said James Earl Ray, alias Eric Starvo Galt, alias John Willard, alias Harvey Lowmeyer, alias Harvey Lowmyer, alias Ramon George Sneyd, committed the offense herein of Murder on the fourth day of April, 1968, in the County of Shelby, the State of Tennessee;

V

That the said James Earl Ray, alias Eric Starvo Galt, alias John Willard, alias Harvey Lowmeyer, alias Harvey Lowmyer, alias Ramon George Sneyd, at the time of the commission of the alleged offense herein of Murder was present in Shelby County and the State of Tennessee, and, that he has thereafter fled from the State of Tennessee, and from the United States of America.

VI

Your Petitioner would further state to Your Excellency, that, at the time of the making of this Petition for Requisition, the said James Earl Ray, alias Eric Starvo Galt, alias John Willard, alias Harvey Lowmeyer, alias Harvey Lowmyer, alias Ramon George Sneyd, has been found within the dominion of the United Kingdom, city of London, England, the grounds for such knowledge, or belief, being the receipt of a telegram from J. Edgar Hoover, Director, Federal Bureau of Investigation, United States of America, that this fugitive has been found and is presently in custody in London, England. There has been no indication that this fugitive will waive extradition.

VII

Transmitted to Your Excellency, the Governor of Tennessee, with this Petition for an Application for the international extradition of this fugitive are the following certified copies of evidence against the said James Earl Ray, alias Eric Starvo Galt, alias John Willard, alias Harvey Lowmeyer, alias Harvey Lowmyer, alias Ramon George Sneyd, consisting of:
1. Certified Copy of the Indictment for Murder
2. Certified Copy of the Capias issued on this Indictment
3. Affidavit of Dr. J. T. Francisco (and Certified Copies)
4. Affidavit of Robert V. Wenzler (and Certified Copies)
5. Affidavit of Guy Warren Canipe, Sr. (and Certified Copies)
6. Affidavit of Inspector N. E. Zachary (and Certified

Copies)
7. Affidavit of Capt. R. L. Williams (and Certified Copies)
8. Affidavit of Cordra York, Sr. (and Certified Copies)
9. Affidavit of Lt. James D. Hamby (and Certified Copies)
10. Certification of the Law of Tennessee in regard to Murder
11. Certified Copy of the Death Certificate
12. Certified Copy of the Autopsy Report (Protocol)
13. Affidavit of Robert G. Jensen, Special Agent in Charge, Federal Bureau of Investigation (and Certified Copies)

VIII

Your Petitioner would, also, further state to Your Excellency, that, this Petition for extradition is presented solely for the purpose of bringing about the trial and punishment of James Earl Ray, alias Eric Starvo Galt, alias John Willard, alias Harvey Lowmeyer, alias Harvey Lowmyer, alias Ramon George Sneyd, and not for any private purpose, and that if the extradition is granted, the criminal proceedings will not be used for any private purpose.

Wherefore, your petition prays: That an Application issue to the Secretary of the State of the United States of America for the international extradition of James Earl Ray, alias Eric Starvo Galt, alias John Willard, alias Harvey Lowmeyer, alias Harvey Lowmyer, alias Ramon George Sneyd, from the United Kingdom to the United States of America and to the State of Tennessee, to-wit: Shelby County, for trial on the indictment charging him with Murder, now pending against him in the Criminal Courts of Shelby County, Tennessee.

[Signed] Phil M. Canale, Jr.
District Attorney General
Fifteenth Judicial Circuit
State of Tennessee

STATE OF TENNESSEE
COUNTY OF SHELBY

I, Phil M. Canale, Jr., solemnly swear that the facts set forth in the foregoing Petition are true, except those allegations made on information, and belief, which are true to the best of my knowledge and belief.

[Signed] Phil M. Canale, Jr.

STATE OF TENNESSEE
COUNTY OF SHELBY

Before me J. A. Blackwell, Clerk of the Criminal Courts of the Shelby County, Tennessee, being an officer constituted to take oaths, appeared Phil M. Canale, Jr., to me known personally and after being duly sworn, stated that the foregoing petition and oath are true and correct to the best of his knowledge, information, and belief. I hereby certify that this document is the original petition and oath of Phil M. Canale, Jr.

In testimony whereof I have hereunto set my hand and affixed the seal of said Court, at office, in the City of Memphis, this 10th day of June, 1968.

[Signed] J. A. Blackwell, Clerk

STATE OF TENNESSEE
COUNTY OF SHELBY

I, Perry H. Sellers, sole and presiding Judge of Criminal Court of said County Division I, certify that J. A. Blackwell, whose true and genuine signature appears above to the foregoing certificate, is now, and was at the time of signing the same, Clerk of said Court, and that said Court is a Court of Record; that his attestation is in due form, and his official acts, as such, are entitled to full faith and credit.

Witness my hand, this 10th day of June, 1968.

[Signed] Perry H. Sellers, Judge

STATE OF TENNESSEE
COUNTY OF SHELBY

I, J. A. Blackwell, Clerk of the Criminal Courts of said County, certify that Honorable Perry H. Sellers, whose genuine official signature appears to the above and hereto annexed Certificate, is and was at the time of signing the same, sole and presiding Judge of the Criminal Court Division I, in and for the County and State aforesaid, duly commissioned and qualified, and that all his official acts, as such, are entitled to full faith and credit.

In testimony whereof I have hereunto set my hand and affixed the seal of said Court, at office, in the City of Memphis this 10th day of June, 1968.

[Signed] J. A. Blackwell, Clerk

No. 1 6 6 4 5

STATE OF TENNESSEE
INDICTMENT FOR

MURDER IN THE FIRST DEGREE

VS.
- JAMES EARL RAY, alias
- "ERIC STARVO GALT", alias
- "JOHN WILLARD", alias
- "HARVEY LOMMEYER", alias
- "HARVEY LOWMYER"

WITNESSES:
Summon for State

Bessie Ruth Brewer	422-1/2 S. Main
Ralph Carpenter	c/o York Arms Co. 162 S.Main
Guy W. Canipe	424 S. Main or 1028 Brower
John L. Carlisle-Criminal Investigator, Attorney	General's Office
Inspector N.E.Zachary c/o Police Dept.	
Lieut.J.L. Harrison-c/o Police Dept.	

By order of

PHIL M. CANALE, JR.
Attorney-General

Sworn by the Foreman of the Grand Jury
to give evidence on this Bill of Indictment
on this, the 7th day of MAY 19 68

W.F.BOWLD
Foreman of the Grand Jury

J.L.HARRISON
Prosecutor

A TRUE BILL

W.F.BOWLD
Foreman of the Grand Jury.

15

INDICTMENT OF JAMES EARL RAY
FOR THE MURDER OF
MARTIN LUTHER KING, JR.

STATE OF TENNESSEE
SHELBY COUNTY

Criminal Court of Shelby County
January Term, A.D. 1968

The Grand Jurors of the State of Tennessee, duly elected, empaneled, sworn and charged to inquire in and for the body of the County of Shelby, in the State aforesaid, upon their oath, present that James Earl Ray, alias, "Eric Starvo Galt," alias "John Willard," alias "Harvey Lowmeyer," alias "Harvey Lowmyer," late of the County aforesaid, heretofore, to-wit on the 4th day of April, A.D. 1968 before the finding of this indictment, in the County aforesaid, did unlawfully, feloniously, willfully, deliberately, premeditatedly and of his malice aforethought kill and murder Martin Luther King, Jr., against the peace and dignity of the State of Tennessee.

Phil M. Canale, Jr.
Attorney General
Criminal Court of Shelby County, Tennessee

16

INDICTMENT, A TRUE BILL, RETURNED BY THE
GRAND JURY OF SHELBY COUNTY,TENNESSEE,
UNDER DATE OF MAY 7th, 1968-VS.JAMES EARL
RAY,alias "ERIC STARVO GALT,"alias "HARVEY
LOWMEYER",alias "HARVEY LOWMYER",SUBJECT
NOT IN CUSTODY IN STATE OF TENNESSEE

No. 16645

To   M A Y   Term, 19 68

STATE OF TENNESSEE

vs.

CAPIAS

JAMES EARL RAY,alias "ERIC STARVO
GALT",alias "JOHN WILLARD",alias
"HARVEY LOWMEYER",alias "HARVEY
LOWMYER"

Issued 7th day of   MAY   19 68

Came to hand_____day of_____19_____

Defendant arrested_____day

of _____19_____

and_____

_____

_____

Sheriff Shelby County.

By _____

Deputy Sheriff Shelby County.

17

685403

STATE OF TENNESSEE

To All Sheriffs of State of Tennessee—GREETING:

You Are Hereby Commanded to take the body of _____
JAMES EARL RAY, alias "ERIC STARVO GALT", alias "JOHN WILLARD", alias "HARVEY LOWMEYER", alias "HARVEY LOWMYER" _____ HIM _____
if to be found in your County, and _____ safely keep, so that you have _____ HIM _____ before
the Judge of the Criminal Court of Shelby County, at a term of said Court, to be held for the County of Shelby,
at the Court House in Memphis, on the third Monday in _____ M A Y _____ 19 68 _____
then and there to answer the State of Tennessee, on _____ A _____ Bill of Indictment, against HIM _____ for

_____ MURDER IN THE FIRST DEGREE _____

_____

Herein fail not and have you then and there this Writ.

Witness, J. A. BLACKWELL, Clerk of said Court, at office, in Memphis, the third Monday in _____

_____ Term 19 68 _____

J. A. BLACKWELL, Clerk

_____ D. C.

18

THE LAW OF
THE STATE OF TENNESSEE
IN REGARD TO MURDER
IN THE FIRST DEGREE

STATE OF TENNESSEE
DEPARTMENT OF STATE

To all to whom these Presents shall come. Greeting:

I, Joe C. Carr, Secretary of State of the State of Tennessee, do hereby certify that the annexed is a true copy of Sections 39-2401, 39-2402 and 39-2405 of Chapter No. 24, Tennessee Code Annotated, and are a full embodiment of the statutory law in regard to murder in the first degree and the punishment therefor as the law existed on April 4, 1968 and on May 7, 1968, the original of which is now on file and a matter of record in this office.

Chapter 24
HOMICIDE

39-2401. MURDER: if any person of sound memory and discretion, unlawfully kill any reasonable creature in being, and under the peace of the state, with malice aforethought, either express or implied, such person shall be guilty of murder. [Code 1858, sect. 4597 (deriv. Acts 1829, ch. 23, sect. 2); Shan., sect. 6438; Code 1932, sect. 10767.]

39-2402. MURDER IN THE FIRST DEGREE: Every murder perpetrated by means of poison, lying in wait, or by any other kind of willful, deliberate, malicious, and premeditated killing, or committed in the perpetration of, or attempt to perpetrate, any murder in the first degree, arson, rape, robbery, burglary, or larceny, is murder in the first degree. [Code 1858, sect. 4598 (deriv. Acts 1829, ch. 23, sect. 3); Shan., sect. 6439; mod. Code 1932, sect. 10768].

39-2405. PUNISHMENT FOR MURDER IN THE FIRST DEGREE: Every person convicted of murder in the first degree, or as accessory before the fact to such crime, shall suffer death by electrocution, or be imprisoned for life or over twenty (20) years, as the jury may determine. [Code 1858, sect. 4601 (deriv. Acts 1829, ch. 23, sect. 4); Acts 1913 (1st E. S.), Shan., sect. 6442; Acts 1919, ch. 4, sect. 1; 1919, ch. 5, sects. 2, 3; Code 1932, sect. 10771.]

In testimony thereof, I have hereunto surscribed my Official Signature and by order of the Governor affixed the Great Seal of the State of Tennessee at the Department in the City of Nashville, this 10th day of June, A.D. 1968.

[Signed] Joe C. Carr
Secretary of State

AFFIDAVIT OF DR. J. T. FRANCISCO

Now comes the affiant, after first being duly sworn and says as follows:

That he is Dr. J. T. Francisco and resides and is domiciled at 1196 Yorkshire, Memphis, Shelby County, Tennessee, United States of America; that he is employed by the University of Tennessee as a pathologist and by Shelby County, Tennessee, as Medical Examiner for Shelby County, Tennessee; that he is a duly licensed and practicing physician of the State of Tennessee and holds a Doctor of Medicine Degree from the University of Tennessee and has practiced medicine for thirteen years and has served as medical examiner for Shelby County, Tennessee, for seven years.

That as part of his duties as medical examiner, he examines all violent, unusual, or unnatural deaths that occur within the County of Shelby, State of Tennessee, for purposes of discovering the cause of death and recommending autopsies upon such deaths investigated if he deems it necessary. During his seven years as medical examiner, affiant has examined approximately nine thousand bodies and performed approximately three thousand autopsies. Affiant is further certified by the American Board of Pathology in Anatomic, Clinical and Forensic Pathology. That affiant is forensic pathology consultant to the Chief Medical Examiner of the State of Tennessee.

That on April 4, 1968, acting pursuant to his duties as medical examiner of Shelby County, Tennessee, and under order from the District Attorney General for the Fifteenth Judicial Circuit consisting of Shelby County, Tennessee, said District Attorney General being Phil M. Canale, Jr., and with the consent of Corretta Scott King, the widow of Dr. Martin Luther King, Jr., affiant performed an autopsy on the body of Dr. Martin Luther King, Jr., starting at approximately 2140 hours at the morgue of the University of Tennessee and John Gaston Hospital, located in the Institute of Pathology at the University of Tennessee, 858 Madison Avenue, Memphis, Shelby County, Tennessee.

That during the examination and autopsy, affiant removed a bullet from beneath the skin in the region of the left scapula 56 inches superior to the right heel and 3 inches to the left of the midline of the spine, this being the termination point of a bullet that entered the right chin, passing through the chin and neck.

That after removing the bullet, affiant physically marked the bullet by scratching the Autopsy No. 252 on the base thereof, and placed the same in plastic and enclosed the same in a Manila envelope, marking thereon and gave the same into the custody and gathering a written receipt from Lt. J. D. Hamby of Memphis, Tennessee, Police Department.

In accordance with the laws of the State of Tennessee, affiant did reduce the findings from the autopsy he performed upon the body of Dr. Martin Luther King, Jr., to writing in the form of an autopsy report bearing Case No. A68-252, did sign same under date of April 11, 1968, and filed said autopsy report with the Shelby County Medical Examiner, District Attorney General of the Fifteenth Judicial Circuit comprised by Shelby County, Tennessee, and with Chief Medical Examiner for the State of Tennessee.

Affiant has examined a copy of the aforesaid autopsy report, which is attached and marked exhibit hereto, a certified and authenticated copy of which appears, is attached and is made by reference a part of the Governor's application for requisition, and certifies that it truely and accurately represents his findings in the autopsy of the body of Dr. Martin Luther King, Jr., and further certifies that it is a true and correct copy of the autopsy report filed with the Office of the Chief Medical Examiner for the State of Tennessee, Cordell Hull Office Building, Division of Post Mortem Examination, Office of Chief Medical Examiner, Nashville, Tennessee.

That affiant has examined Certificate of Death, Tennessee Department of Public Health, Division of Vital Statistics, bearing File No. 2066, being a copy of the Certificate of Death on Dr. Martin Luther King, Jr., same being attached and marked exhibit hereto, a certified and authenticated copy of which appears, is attached and is made by reference a part of the Governor's application for requisition, and does certify that it represents a true and correct copy of the original Certificate of Death on Dr. Martin Luther King, Jr., signed by affiant on April 5, 1968, giving the cause of death as gunshot wound to the thoracic cord.

Affiant has examined survey report and plat, identified to affiant as being a drawing of the crime scene, said document bearing the notation in the lower right hand corner, Prepared by Arthur C. Holbrook, Memphis, Tennessee, April 23, 1968, Tenn. Cert. No. 5173, copy of said drawing being attached and made exhibit hereto, a certified and authenticated copy of which appears, is attached and is made by reference a part of the Governor's application for requisition, and affirms that the trajectory of a bullet traveling along the path as indicated in said drawing would be consistent with the entry of the bullet and subsequent course through the body of Dr. Martin Luther King, Jr.

Further affiant sayeth not.

[Signed] Dr. J. T. Francisco
1196 Yorkshire
Memphis, Shelby County, Tennessee
United States of America

23

STATE OF TENNESSEE
COUNTY OF SHELBY

Before me J. A. Blackwell, Clerk of the Criminal Courts of Shelby County, Tennessee, being an officer constituted to take oaths, appeared Dr. J. T. Francisco, to me known personally and after being duly sworn, stated that the foregoing affidavit of three pages is true and correct to the best of his knowledge, information, and belief. I hereby certify that this document is the original affidavit of Dr. J. T. Francisco.

In testimony whereof I have hereunto set my hand and affixed the seal of said Court, at office, in the City of Memphis, this 10th day of June, 1968.

[Signed] J. A. Blackwell, Clerk

PROVISIONAL ( )

FINAL (X)

TENNESSEE DEPARTMENT OF PUBLIC HEALTH

OFFICE OF THE CHIEF MEDICAL EXAMINER

858 Madison Avenue
Memphis, Tennessee 38103

CASE NO. A68-252

COUNTY Shelby

AUTOPSY REPORT

NAME OF DECEDENT __Martin Luther King, Jr.__   RACE _N_ SEX _M_ AGE _39_

HOME ADDRESS _____ __Atlanta, Georgia__ _____
              NUMBER OR STREET   CITY OR TOWN   STATE

COUNTY MEDICAL EXAMINER ___J. T. Francisco, M.D._____

ADDRESS __Memphis, Tennessee_____

DISTRICT ATTORNEY GENERAL __Phil A. Canale_____

ADDRESS __Memphis, Tennessee_____

ANATOMICAL DIAGNOSIS · __Gunshot wound to body and face with:_____
              Fracture of mandible
              Laceration vertebral artery, jugular vein and sub-
              clavian artery, right,
              Laceration of spinal cord (lower cervical, upper
                                        thoracic),
              Intrapulmonary hematoma, apex, right upper lobe

CAUSE OF DEATH __Gunshot wound to spinal column, lower cervical, upper__
        thoracic

NARRATIVE OF FINDINGS __Death was the result of a gunshot wound to the__
chin and neck with a total transection of the lower cervical and
upper thoracic spinal cord and other structures in the neck. The
direction of the wounding was from front to back, above downward and
from right to left. The severing of the spinal cord at this level
and to this extent was a wound that was fatal very shortly after its
occurrence.

   The purpose of this report is to provide a certified opinion to the County Medical
Examiner and the District Attorney General. The facts and findings to support these con-
clusions are filed with the office of the State Medical Examiner.

DATE __April 11, 1968__ SIGNATURE: _____ M.D.
                                        J. T. Francisco
              ADDRESS __858 Madison Avenue-Memphis, Tennessee__

MEMPHIS AND SHELBY COUNTY HEALTH DEPARTMENT :: 814 JEFFERSON AVENUE, MEMPHIS, TENNESSEE 38105

CERTIFICATE OF DEATH
TENNESSEE DEPARTMENT OF PUBLIC HEALTH
DIVISION OF VITAL STATISTICS

FILE NO. **2066**

1. DECEASED — NAME — FIRST	Martin
MIDDLE	Luther
LAST	King, Jr.
2. DATE OF DEATH	4-4-68
3. SEX	Male
4. COLOR OR RACE	Negro
5a. AGE — LAST BIRTHDAY (YEARS)	39
5b. UNDER 1 YEAR — MOS. DAYS	
5c. UNDER 1 DAY — HOURS MIN.	
6. DATE OF BIRTH	1-15-29
7a. STATE OF BIRTH (IF NOT IN U.S.A., NAME COUNTRY)	Georgia
7b. CITIZEN OF WHAT COUNTRY	America
7c. HOSPITAL OR OTHER INSTITUTION — NAME	St. Joseph Hospital
7d. IF HOSPITAL, GIVE CITY, TOWN OR LOCATION	Memphis
8. SOCIAL SECURITY NUMBER	253-36-3980
9. USUAL OCCUPATION	Minister & Civil Rights Leader
9a. KIND OF BUSINESS OR INDUSTRY	So. Christian Leadership Conference
10. MARRIED, NEVER MARRIED, WIDOWED, DIVORCED	Married
11. SURVIVING SPOUSE	Coretta King (nee Scott)
12a. RESIDENCE — STATE	Georgia
12b. COUNTY	Fulton
12c. CITY, TOWN, OR LOCATION	Atlanta
12d. STREET AND NUMBER	234 Sunset N.W.
16. FATHER — NAME	Martin L. King, Sr.
17. MOTHER — MAIDEN NAME	Alberta Williams
18a. INFORMANT — NAME	Coretta King, 234 Sunset N.W., Ga.

PART I. DEATH WAS CAUSED BY:

IMMEDIATE CAUSE (a) Gunshot Wound to Thoracic Cord

CONDITIONS, IF ANY, WHICH GAVE RISE TO IMMEDIATE CAUSE (a), STATING THE UNDERLYING CAUSE LAST.
DUE TO, OR AS A CONSEQUENCE OF:
(b)
DUE TO, OR AS A CONSEQUENCE OF:
(c)

PART II. OTHER SIGNIFICANT CONDITIONS: CONDITIONS CONTRIBUTING TO DEATH BUT NOT RELATED TO CAUSE GIVEN IN PART I (a)

19a. ACCIDENT, SUICIDE, HOMICIDE	Homicide
20a. DATE OF INJURY	4-4-68
20b. HOUR	6 P. M.
20c. (INJURY AT WORK)	No
20d. PLACE OF INJURY	Motel
20e. LOCATION	406 Mulberry, Memphis, Tennessee
21. HOW INJURY OCCURRED	Victim was shot.
22. AUTOPSY	Yes
23. CERTIFIER	J. T. Francisco, M.D.
23b. DATE SIGNED	4-5-68
25. BURIAL, CREMATION, REMOVAL	Removal
25a. DATE	4-5-68
25b. CEMETERY OR CREMATORY	Southview
25c. LOCATION	Atlanta, Georgia
26. FUNERAL HOME — NAME AND ADDRESS	R. S. Lewis Funeral Home, 374 Vance Avenue

AUTOPSY PROTOCOL
The City of Memphis Hospitals

Autopsy No: A68-252
Service: Med. Ex.
Name: Martin Luther King, Jr.
Age: 39
Race: Negro
Sex: Male
Date of Admission: DOA
Date and Hour of Death: Unknown—Approximately
    4/4/68 p.m.
Date and Hour of Autopsy: 4/4/68 10:45 p.m.
Pathologists: Drs. Sprunt and Francisco
Date completed: 4/11/68

FINAL PATHOLOGICAL DIAGNOSIS

PRIMARY SERIES:
    I.   Distant gunshot wound to body and face
        A. Fracture of right mandible
        B. Laceration of vertebral artery, jugular vein and subclavian artery, right
        C. Fracture of spine (T-1, C-7)
        D. Laceration of spinal cord (lower cervical, upper thoracic)
        E. Submucosal hemorrhage, larynx
        F. Intrapulmonary hematoma, apex right upper lobe

SECONDARY SERIES:
1. Remote scars as described
2. Pleural adhesions
3. Fatty change liver, moderate
4. Arteriosclerosis, moderate
5. Venous cut-downs
6. Tracheostomy

LABORATORY FINDINGS:
Blood Alcohol: 0.01%

EXTERNAL EXAMINATION OF THE BODY

This is a well developed, well nourished Negro male measuring 69½ inches in length and weighing approximately 140 pounds. The hair is black, the eyes are brown. There is a line mustache present.

EXTERNAL MARKS AND SCARS

There is a remote midline scar present in the center of the chest and a remote scar present extending to the right axilla measuring 8 inches in length. There is a sutured vertical surgical incision present at the base of the neck. A sutured incision is present in the right chest at the anterior axillary line. Three needle punctures are present in the precordium, having no hemorrhage present surrounding the area. There are blood splatters present on the palm and dorsum of the right hand. A remote scar is present in the right lateral chest. Sutured incisions are present in the left ante cubital fossa, one that is obliquely directed measuring 2 inches in length, one that is horizontally directed measuring 1 inch in length. There are two sutured incisions present on the medial aspect of the left ankle. The superior incision measuring 2 inches in length, the inferior incision measuring ¼ inch in length. There is an extensive excavating lesion affecting the right side of the face beginning at a point 1 inch lateral to the right corner of the mouth and ½ inch inferior to the right corner of the mouth that measures approximately 3 inches in length. At the superior aspect of this gaping wound there is an abrasion collar that measures 1/8 of an inch in maximum thickness, having brownish discoloration present at the superior margin. Adjacent to this area there is extensive laceration of the soft tissues of the face with a fracturing of the right side of the mandible. A re-approximation of the tissues reveals the laceration to extend to the base of the neck and into the base of the neck with intervening skin unaffected in this area. The second penetrating wound at the base of the neck in the superior aspect of the chest measures 3 inches in length. The missile path is through the external jugular vein and vertebral artery. There is a penetration into the lateral aspect of the base of the neck into the upper thoracic and lower cervical cord totally severing the lower cervical and upper thoracic cord passing through the spinal column at the level of C7 and T1 into the posterior aspect of the back. The bullet is removed from the posterior aspect of the back, 56 inches superior to the right heel and 55½ inches superior to the left heel, 3 inches to the left of the midline of the spine in the medial aspect of the left scapula. The entrance wound is 61½ inches superior to the right heel and 59 inches superior to the right heel with the head turned and positioned so that the wound in the face corresponds with the path of the missile into the neck and spine. The total thickness from the entrance wound to the posterior aspect of the back is 8½ inches in thickness. The angle of the penetrating wound is approximately 45 degrees from a sagittal plane about a 30-degree angle with the coronal plane.

SECTION

The abdominal panniculus measures an inch in maximum thickness. The skeletal muscles are red and fibillary. There is scarring present over the right anterior-superior chest with pleural adhesions present in this area.

BODY CAVITIES

There is approximately 25cc. of blood present within the right thoracic cavity and some subpleural hemorrhage that is present affecting the right and the left in the posterior apex. The missile did not enter the right pleural cavity.

GROSS DESCRIPTION OF THE ORGANS

HEART: The heart weighs 450 grams. The myocardium is pale brown. The valvular surfaces reveal no significant changes. There is focal yellowing of the subendocardial areas affecting the left aspect of the interventricular septum. The right ventricle measures 5mm. in maximum thickness. The left ventricle measures 20mm. in maximum thickness. The coronary ostia originate in normal position and have a normal distribution over the epicardial surface. There is minimal intimal proliferation present. Focal yellow plaqueing is present in the ascending aspect of the aortic arch but ulceration is not present. There is no significant dilatation affecting the chambers of the heart.

AORTA: Focal yellow plaques are present throughout the aorta but ulceration and calcification is not present. The great vessels originate normally. There is perivascular hemorrhage affecting the right carotid artery but no penetration of the wall. The right subclavian artery is lacerated.

ESOPHAGUS: Partially digested food fragments are present throughout the esophagus.

TRACHEA: Hemorrhagic mucoid material is present throughout the upper trachea.

LUNGS: The right lung weighs 300 grams. The left lung weighs 325 grams. There is diffuse congestion, consolidation and hemorrhage affecting the right upper lobe of the lung. Frothy fluid is expressable from the sectioned surface. There is minimal wrinkling of the pleura diffusely throughout the pulmonary parenchyma.

BRAIN: The brain weighs 1400 grams. There is some flattening of the gyri and narrowing of the sulci. The cerebral vessels are symmetrical. There is no subdural, epidural, or extradural hemorrhage present. There is no significant flattening throughout the cerebral vessels.

KIDNEYS: The kidneys weigh 175 grams on the left and 150 grams on the right. The capsular surface is smooth. The parenchyma is of normal coloration. The cortical-medullary junction is prominent.

PANCREAS: The pancreatic parenchyma is well preserved. The lobular pattern is preserved. There is no fatty infiltration present. The parenchyma is yellowish-grey.

LARYNX: There is diffuse hemorrhage present throughout the superior larynx along with submucosal hemorrhage that is present within the intra-laryngeal areas. There is a tracheostomy perforation that is superior to the thyroid penetrating to the right of the pyramidal lobe.

THYROID: No significant changes.

SPLEEN: The spleen weighs 80 grams. The capsule is wrinkled. There is no capsular thickening present. The follicles are not prominent.

STOMACH: The stomach contains approximately 10cc. of partially digested food fragments. There is no ulceration present.

DUODENUM: No significant changes.

GALLBLADDER: The gallbladder contains approximately 5cc. of light green bile. No stones are present.

LIVER: The liver weighs 1600 grams. The parenchyma is pale yellowish-brown. The lobular pattern is accentuated. The parenchyma is quite soft.

BLADDER: There is approximately 25cc. of cloudy yellow urine present.

PROSTATE: No significant gross abnormalities are present.

COLON: The appendix is present. The colonic contents is normal.

SMALL INTESTINE: There is alternately liquid and gaseous distention present throughout the small intestine.

ADRENALS: The adrenals are in normal position and weigh 8 grams together. The cortex is bright yellow. The medulla is grey.

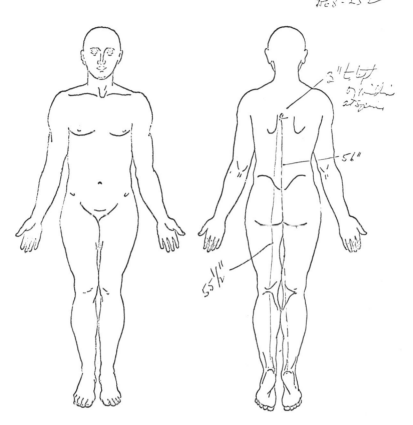

3" t lt
of spine
at spine

56"

55½"

33

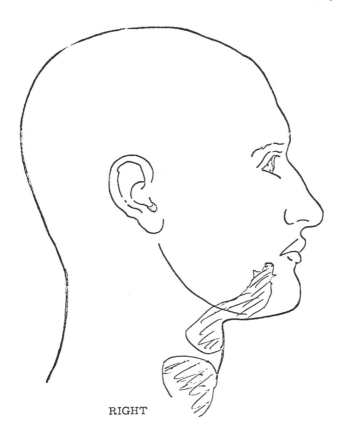

RIGHT

34

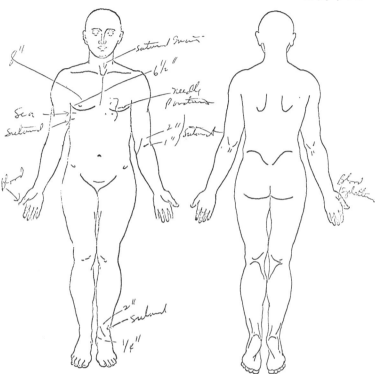

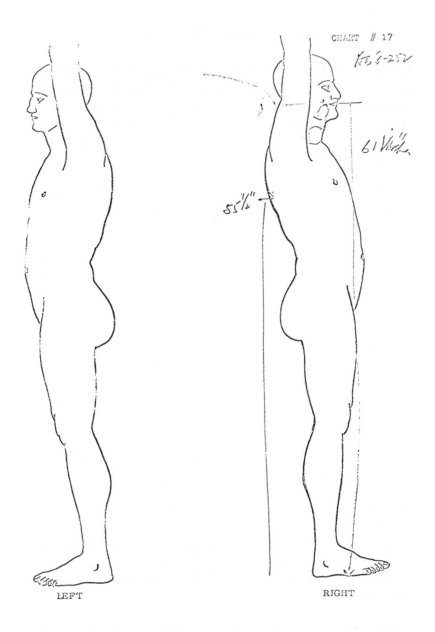

CHART # 17

N 8-252

61 1/2"

55 1/2"

LEFT   RIGHT

36

MICROSCOPIC SUMMARY

LUNG: Focal areas of intra-alveolar hemorrhage are present throughout. Otherwise the alveoli are well preserved without hyperdistention or collapse. There is a loss of bronchial epithelium free within the lumens of the bronchioles. The pulmonary vessels reveal no significant changes.

PANCREAS: The pancreatic parenchyma is well preserved. The islets and acini are well preserved. There is minimal congestion present but no fibrosis or hemorrhage.

KIDNEY: The glomeruli and tubules are well preserved. There is no parenchymal fibrosis evident or vascular proliferation present. The tubules are filled with eosinophilic material. There is no collapse of the tubular lumen.

THYROID: The follicles are uniform and regular. There is a small quantity of extravasation of mature erythrocytes into peri-follicular locations. Cellular inflammatory reaction is not present. There is no margination of polymorphonuclear leucocytes within the areas of hemorrhage.

LIVER: There is diffuse cytoplasmic vacuolation throughout the hepatic cytoplasm being distributed throughout the lobules and in both pericentral and periportal locations. A small number of mononuclear cells are present in portal areas. There is some variation in size, shape of the hepatic nuclei. The vacuoles that are present are irregular in size, being numerous in some cells and being single large vacuoles in others with a disruption of cytoplasmic borders in some.

ADRENAL: There is congestion of the inner cortical zones of the adrenal. The cytoplasm is otherwise well maintained. The cortico-medullary ratio is maintained.

SPLEEN: The follicles are present but without secondary reactive centers. There is some congestion of the pulp but focal hemorrhage is not present.

HEART: The mycardial fibers are well preserved. The nuclei are regular. Fibrosis is not present throughout the myocardium and cellular inflammatory reaction is not present. The atrium reveals no significant changes.

SKIN: There is dermal hemorrhage present but no accumulation of polymorphonuclear leucocytes. Blackened debris is present throughout the hemorrhagic area of the dermis having no identifiable form. There is pronounced eosinophilia of the collagen bundles. There is hemorrhage into the dermal layers with an alteration in the tinctorial properties of the epithelium with focal fragmentation of the epithelium adjacent to the area of dermal hemorrhage.

CORONARY: There is moderate intimal proliferation along with an extra cellular deposition of lipid within the subintimal areas along with lipid filled macrophages present in this location. Small foci of perivascular mononuclear cells are present in the regions of most pronounced intimal proliferation.

PROSTATE: The glandular elements are well preserved without any significant increase in collageneous connective tissue. Inflammatory reaction is not present.

CERTIFICATION

I, Thomas C. Littlejohn, Jr., Chief Medical Examiner for the State of Tennessee, do hereby certify that this is a true and perfect copy of the autopsy report, the original of which is now on file and a matter of record in this office.

[Signed] Thomas C. Littlejohn, Jr.
Chief Medical Examiner, State of Tennessee

STATE OF TENNESSEE
DEPARTMENT OF STATE

I, Joe C. Carr, Secretary of State of the State of Tennessee do hereby certify that Thomas C. Littlejohn, Jr., is the Chief Medical Examiner for the State of Tennessee and the person authorized to certify Autopsy Reports in the State of Tennessee.

I further certify that to the best of my knowledge and belief the signature on the attached Autopsy Report is the true and genuine signature of Thomas C. Littlejohn, Jr., Chief Medical Examiner for the State of Tennessee.

In witness whereof, I have hereto affixed my signature and the Great Seal of the State, at Nashville, this 10th day of June in the year of our Lord nineteen hundred and sixty-eight.

[Signed] Joe C. Carr
Secretary of State

AFFIDAVIT OF ROBERT V. WENZLER

Affiant, after first being duly sworn, says as follows:

That he is Robert V. Wenzler, residing at 4100 Ward Avenue, Memphis, Shelby County, Tennessee, United States of America, and that on April 23, 1968, he was employed by the City of Memphis, Tennessee as Senior Party Chief in the Engineering Department in the Department of Public Works of Memphis, Shelby County, Tennessee, that as Senior Party Chief, his duties consisted of making Field Computations, Civil Engineering Surveys, and Construction Layouts, that he has had over fifteen (15) years experience as a surveyor with related Civil Engineering duties, that on April 23, 1968, he, along with Arthur C. Holbrook, Engineer of Surveys, Plans, and Designs, similarly employed by the Engineering Department of the Public Works Department of the City of Memphis, Tennessee, on request of the City of Memphis Fire and Police Director, met with Lts. J.L. Harrison and A.S. Zelinski, of the Homicide Division of the Memphis Police Department, and conducted a survey of the area where Dr. Martin Luther King, Jr. was slain, to determine by the method of triangulation the distance, trajectory, and path from the point of the death bullet's alledged origination to the point of impact upon the body of Dr. Martin Luther King, Jr.

The survey party consisted of affiant, the aforesaid Arthur C. Holbrook, another Party Chief, one instrument man, and three (3) engineering aids. All measurements and angles were reduced to writing by affiant and Arthur C. Holbrook from which computations were subsequently made and transposed into a plat, faithfully and correctly reflecting the measurements and angles taken on the aforesaid date. Affiant has examined exhibit attached hereto consisting of a survey report with plat attached thereto, dated April 23, 1968, addressed to Frank C. Holloman, Director of Fire and Police of the City of Memphis, Tennessee, and signed Arthur C. Holbrook, Engineer of Surveys, Plans, and Designs, Tennessee License No.5173, and the same is a true and correct copy of the survey conducted by affiant, pursuant to his duties on April 23, 1968.

Further affiant saith not.

STATE OF TENNESSEE
COUNTY OF SHELBY

Before me J. A. Blackwell, Clerk of the Criminal Courts of Shelby County, Tennessee, being an officer constituted to take oaths, appeared Robert V. Wenzler, to me known personally and after being duly sworn, stated that the foregoing affidavit of one page is true and correct to the best of his knowledge, information and belief. I hereby certify that this document is the original affidavit of Robert V. Wenzler.

In testimony whereof I have hereunto set my hand and affixed the seal of said Court, at office, in the City of Memphis, this 10th day of June, 1968.

[Signed] J. S. Blackwell, Clerk

EXHIBIT TO AFFIDAVIT OF ROBERT V. WENZLER

CITY OF MEMPHIS
DIVISION OF PUBLIC WORKS
Charles B. Blackburn, Director

April 23, 1968

Mr. Frank C. Holloman, Director
Division of Fire and Police
City of Memphis, Memphis, Tennessee

Dear Mr. Holloman:

Per your request, dated April 22, 1968, through Mr. Charles B. Blackburn, Director, Division of Public Works, I was instructed to make certain engineering measurements relative to the murder of Dr. Martin Luther King. These measurements were to be from a point where the weapon was fired to the area where Dr. King was· struck. The measurements were to be triangulated.

This morning, April 23, 1968, I and several engineering employees from this department, met with Lts. A. S. Zelinski and J. L. Harrison, of the Police Department, at the scene of the murder. The measurements and calculations, hereinafter described, were made between 8:30 a.m. and 10 a.m., this date.

I was shown, by Lts. Zelinski and Harrison, the spot where Dr. King was standing and the window from which the shot was fired and that the bullet entered Dr. King at a point 59 inches above the balcony floor of the Lorraine Motel, and that the gun was resting on a point on a windowsill of a building which fronts on South Main Street and across Mulberry Street from the Lorraine Motel.

An engineer's transit was placed over the spot where Dr. King was shot. The telescope being 59 inches from the balcony floor, and the instrument was made level.

From this position two triangles were established, with a base line common to the two triangles, established and measured. Angles were turned, checked, turned again, and checked again and every effort was made to provide for the utmost accuracy of the calculations.

The level distance from the point from which the shot was fired to the point where Dr. King was standing is 206.36 feet. The distance along the flight of the bullet from the point from which it was fired to the point where Dr. King was standing is 207.02 feet.

The windowsill of the building from which the shot was fired is 16.63 feet higher than a point 59 inches above the floor of the balcony on which Dr. King was standing when shot.

In addition to the aforementioned Lts. Zelinski and Harrison, the following named men from this department were present and assisted in this survey, and statistics relative to these men furnished in the following order: Name, title, age, length of service with this department, address, and home phone number.

Arthur C. Holbrook; Engineer of Surveys, Plans, & Design; 52 years old; 22 years 5 months; 3730 Shirlwood Avenue; 323-8853.

Robert V. Wenzler; Senior Party Chief; 32; 15 years 8 months; 4100 Ward Avenue; 386-7766.

Aaron Russell; Senior Party Chief; 54; 28 years 6 months; 2119 Alta Vista Drive; 357-3819.

Billy Fite; Instrumentman; 35; 11 years; 2208 Cassie Avenue; 357-4522.

Joe Tidwell; Engineering Aide; 21; 1 year 7 months; 1992 Driftwood Avenue; 357-3804.

Thomas Boillot; Engineering Aide; 24; 7 months; 2085 Linden Avenue; 278-0504.

Charles Brooks; Engineering Aide; 18; 5 months;

4608 McCrory Avenue; 685-1223.

I have attached a sketch showing the triangulation as set up at the scene, with angles, measurements, and calculations also shown.

If we can help further in this matter, please advise.

Sincerely,
[Signed] Arthur C. Holbrook, P.E.
Engineer of Surveys, Plans & Design
Tennessee License No. 5173

ACH:dt
Attached

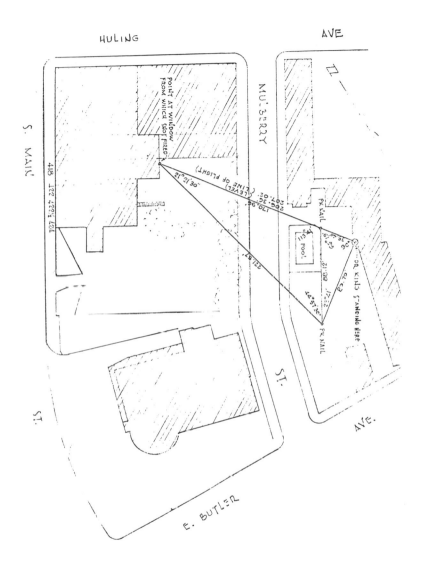

Exhibit to Affidavit of Robert V. Wenzler.

45

AFFIDAVIT OF GUY WARREN CANIPE, SR.

I, Guy Warren Canipe, Sr., being duly sworn depose and say:

1. I reside at 1078 Brower Road, Memphis, Tennessee, and am the owner of the Canipe Amusement Company, 424 South Main Street, Memphis, Tennesee. My store is located immediately adjacent to the rooming house at 422½ South Main Street in Memphis, as depicted in the attached Exhibit I and Exhibit II.

2. My store was closed and unattended most of the day on April 4, 1968, and I returned to it shortly after 5:00 p.m.

3. Sometime around 6:00 I heard a thud in the vicinity of the front door of my store. When I looked up I saw a bundle lying in front of the door to the store. Almost simultaneously, I saw a white man walking from my front door and he apparently turned south on Main Street.

4. I then walked onto the sidewalk to see what had happened to the man who had dropped this bundle. At that time a small white car, in which there was only the driver as occupant, pulled away from the curb just south of my store. I do not know whether the driver was the same man or not that dropped the package, but I did not see the man who dropped the package walking on Main Street at the time the car pulled off.

5. Immediately thereafter, I saw a deputy sheriff walking south on the sidewalk past my store. Other officers arrived immediately after.

6. The attached photograph marked Exhibit III accu-

46

rately portrays the front of my store and the bundle in the place where I found it.

7. The bundle or package appeared to include a large pasteboard box, the top of which was ajar, and from which the portion of a gun barrel was extended. Some type of green cloth was over the top of the bundle. The box had the word "Browning" on it. There was also some type of suitcase or brief case underneath the cloth.

8. The bundle was taken into custody by officers of the Memphis Police Department.

[Signed] Guy Warren Canipe, Sr.

STATE OF TENNESSEE
COUNTY OF SHELBY

Before me J.A. Blackwell, Clerk of the Criminal Courts of Shelby County, Tennessee, being an officer constituted to take oaths, appeared Guy Warren Canipe, Sr., to me known personally and after being duly sworn, stated that the foregoing affidavit of two pages is true and correct to the best of his knowledge, information, and belief. I hereby certify that this document is the original affidavit of Guy Warren Canipe, Sr.

In testimony whereof I have hereunto set my hand and affixed the seal of said Court, at office, in the City of Memphis, this tenth day of June, 1968.

[Signed] J. A. Blackwell, Clerk

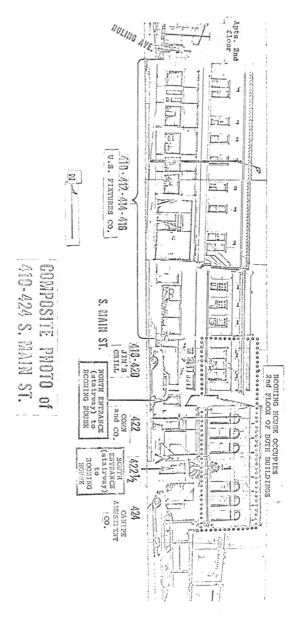

Exhibit I to Affidavit of Guy Warren Canipe, Sr.

Exhibit II to Affidavit of Guy Warren Canipe, Sr.

Exhibit III to Affidavit of Guy Warren Canipe, Sr.

AFFIDAVIT OF INSPECTOR N. E. ZACHARY

Now comes the affiant, N. E. Zachary, after being duly sworn, and states as follows:

That his name is N. E. Zachary, and that he resides at 1507 Old Hickory, Memphis, Shelby County, Tennessee, United States of America, and that he is employed by the Memphis Police Department, in charge of the Homicide Division; that on the date of April 4, 1968, he was so acting and on duty and was assigned to and did conduct and supervise the investigation of the killing of Dr. Martin Luther King, Jr., that as part of the investigation, the affiant personally searched the scene of the killing, and as a result of the search of the scene, at about 6:15 p.m. he personally recovered a certain bundle and articles approximately a block west of the actual spot where Dr. King was slain, specifically being in the doorway of 424 South Main Street, Memphis, Tennessee, this being one door south of the doorway leading from 422½ South Main Street.

That the said bundle and article consisted of a green and brown bedspread measuring 106¼ inches by 85¼ inches and was of a herringbone design; a zipper type bag, which measured 15 inches x 20 inches x 5¼ inches Tel-Star model Japanese make 7x35, Serial Number DQ 408664; a Georgia-Alabama Standard Oil map; copy of the Memphis Commercial Appeal newspaper, first section only, issue of April 4, 1968; a Standard Oil map of the United States; a binocular case with instruction booklet, lens cloth and guarantee card; a yellow cardboard binocular box with black writing; a leather strap-type carrying case; a "Gillette" travel kit, with store label Oliver Rexall Store,

51

Whitehaven, Shelby County, Tennessee, price $1.89, which contained a razor, lotion shaving cream, deodorant, hair cream and razor blade dispenser; grey-blue paper sack bearing "York Arms Company" name with receipt dated 4/4/68 in the amount of $41.55; nine .30-06 Springfield caliber cartridges (five Remington-Peters and 4R-A-55) in Peters cartridge box, Index Number 3033; and two cans of "Schlitz" beer, pull tab type can, along with the plastic six pack carrying device which was in a brown paper sack; along with numerous other miscellaneous toilet articles, underclothing and socks.

Also in this bundle there was a Browning rifle box for a .243 Winchester caliber rifle, Serial Number 4744Z5, which contained a .30-06 Springfield caliber Remington "Gamemaster" slide-action rifle, Model 760, bearing Serial Number 461476, attached to the rifle was a Redfield telescopic sight, which bore Serial Number A17350, and the rifle chamber was seen by me to contain a .30-06 Springfield caliber Remington-Peters empty cartridge case, when examined in my presence by agents of the Federal Bureau of Investigation.

All of the above enumerated articles were confiscated by the affiant in his duties as Inspector of the Memphis, Tennessee, Police Department in the investigation of the slaying of Dr. Martin Luther King, Jr. The said articles from the time of confiscation were in my physical possession and control until on the same date all of the said enumerated articles were given into custody of the Federal Bureau of Investigation of the United States of America, specifically to Robert G. Jensen, Special Agent in charge of the Memphis office of the Federal Bureau of Investigation, and Robert Fitzpatrick, Special Agent of the Memphis office of the Federal Bureau of Investigation, to be personally conveyed by Special Agent Robert Fitzpatrick to the Federal Bureau of Investigation laboratory in Washington, D. C. for criminal analysis.

That on the said date of April 4, 1968, affiant, as part of the investigation, received from one of his officers participating in the investigation, namely, Lieutenant J. D. Hamby, of the Homicide Division of the Memphis Police Department, one battered lead slug, that had been removed from the body of Dr. Martin Luther King, Jr., by the medical examiner, Dr. J. T. Francisco, in Lt. Hamby's presence. This slug particularly marked by Dr. Francisco and enclosed in a small envelope, was given by the affiant, on the same date, into the custody of Cy Bush of the Memphis office of the Federal Bureau of Investigation.

Also found in room 5B that had been rented in the name of John Willard, there were two straps found by Capt. R. L. Williams one of which was black leather, which is 5/8ths of an inch in width and which matched the strap on the binocular case found in the evidence in front of 425 South Main Street, Memphis, Tennessee; also a black leather strap 11/32nds of an inch in width, which attaches to the binoculars for carrying purposes, these straps being confiscated from the room by Capt. R. L. Williams of the Memphis, Tennessee, Police Department and Lieutenant Glen King of the Memphis, Tennessee, Police Department.

On May 3, 1968, the aforementioned evidence was returned to the Memphis office of the Federal Bureau of Investigation and Mr. Robert G. Jensen, Special Agent in charge of the Memphis office of the Federal Bureau of Investigation, turned this evidence back into the custody of the Criminal Court Clerk of Shelby County, Tennessee, at Memphis.

The attached photograph marked Exhibit I accurately portrays the doorway to 424 South Main Street, Memphis, Tennessee, as it was on April 4, 1968, and accurately portrays the location where the bundle was found and confiscated by me, said bundle showing in the photograph being the bundle previously referred to by me in this affidavit, and containing the articles as previously described in this affidavit.

[Signed] N. E. Zachary
Inspector of Detectives
Memphis, Tennessee, Police Department
United States of America

STATE OF TENNESSEE
COUNTY OF SHELBY

Before me J. A. Blackwell, Clerk of the Criminal Courts of Shelby County, Tennessee, being an officer constituted to take oaths, appeared N. E. Zachary, to me known personally and after being duly sworn, stated that the foregoing affidavit of four pages is true and correct to the best of his knowledge, information, and belief. I hereby certify that this document is the original affidavit of N. E. Zachary.

In testimony whereof I have hereunto set my hand and affixed the seal of said Court, at office, in the City of Memphis, this 10th day of June, 1968.

[Signed] J. A. Blackwell, Clerk

Exhibit I to Affidavit of Inspector N. E. Zachary.

55

AFFIDAVIT OF CAPTAIN R. L. WILLIAMS

Affiant first being duly sworn, states as follows:

That he is R. L. Williams, and that he resides at 3549 North Trezevant, Memphis, Shelby County, Tennessee, United States of America, and that he is employed by the Memphis, Tennessee, Police Department, and was so employed on April 4, 1968.

That in his capacity as Captain of the aforesaid Homicide Department, at approximately 6:13 p.m., on April 4, 1968, affiant did make an inspection of the crime scene of the murder of Dr. Martin Luther King, Jr., more particularly described for purposes of this affidavit as a room on the second floor of a rooming house located at 422½ South Main Street, Memphis, Shelby County, Tennessee, said room being identified as Room 5B, rented in the name of John Willard.

That affiant's inspection of the aforesaid room revealed a black leather strap, approximately 11/32nds of an inch in width, was lying on the floor, and a black strap with a metal buckle on the end, being approximately 5/8ths inch in width, was found lying on the couch in said room. That both aforedescribed straps were confiscated as evidence by affiant, and turned over to Inspector N. E. Zachary, affiant's commanding officer, Memphis, Tennessee, Police Department. That affiant has this date examined two straps in the custody of the Criminal Court Clerk of Shelby County, Tennessee, and affirms that such belts are the same as those affiant confiscated as evidence on April 4, 1968, at the place and time heretofore described.

Further affiant saith not.

[Signed] R. L. Williams
Captain, Memphis, Tennessee, Police Department
United States of America

STATE OF TENNESSEE
COUNTY OF SHELBY

Before me J. A. Blackwell, Clerk of the Criminal Courts of Shelby County, Tennessee, being an officer constituted to take oaths, appeared R. L. Williams, to me known personally and after being duly sworn, stated that the foregoing affidavit of one page is true and correct to the best of his knowledge, information, and belief. I hereby certify that this document is the original affidavit of R. L. Williams.

In testimony whereof I have hereunto set my hand and affixed the seal of said Court, at office, in the City of Memphis, this 10th day of June, 1968.

[Signed] J. A. Blackwell, Clerk

AFFIDAVIT OF MR. CORDRA YORK, SR.

Now comes the affiant after first being duly sworn and says as follows:

That he is Cordra York, Sr., and resides at 1365 Yorkshire Drive, Memphis, Shelby County, Tennessee, United States of America; that he is the partner of York Arms Company, a sporting goods business, whose main office is located at 162 South Main, Memphis, Shelby County, Tennessee; that as part of his duty he has custody and control of the business records of the aforesaid company; that as a part of the normal course of business there is carried as normal stock for sale various brands of binoculars and particularly in the normal course of business they carry binoculars known by the brand name of Bushnell binoculars, which are manufactured by the D. P. Bushnell & Company, Inc., of Pasadena, California, United States of America.

An examination of the business records reveals that prior to January 30, 1968, York Arms Company had received three 7x35 Bushnell Banner binoculars to be held in the store for normal sale; and that prior to February 8, 1968, the York Arms Company had received six 7x35 Bushnell Banner binoculars for sale in the normal course of business. That the said binoculars consisted of a binocular leather carrying case and accompanying straps and were contained in a black and yellow cardboard box.

A check of a York Arms cash receipt dated April 4, now in the custody of the Criminal Court Clerk of Shelby County, Tennessee, reveals that on that date a 7x35 Bushnell Banner binocular, with leather case and accompanying straps and a black and yellow cardboard box, was sold for the amount of forty-one dollars and 55/100 ($41.55) for cash and that as a part of the normal procedure such a purchase is placed in a gray-blue paper sack with the writings "York Arms Company" on the outside of the sack. Affiant would further state that he has examined a Bushnell Banner 7x35 binocular with leather case, accompanying straps, yellow and black cardboard box, and gray-blue paper sack, said articles being in the custody of the criminal Court Clerk of Shelby County, Tennessee; and said binocular, with case and accompanying straps and yellow and black box, are of the same manufacture, color, size and similarities of the brand previously described, received, and sold on April 4, 1968, and the gray-blue paper sack is of the same color consistency and make used by affiant's company in the normal course of business.

Further affiant sayeth not.

[Signed] Cordra York, Sr.
1365 Yorkshire Drive
Memphis, Shelby County, Tennessee
United States of America

STATE OF TENNESSEE
COUNTY OF SHELBY

Before me J. A. Blackwell, Clerk of the Criminal Courts of Shelby County, Tennessee, being an officer constituted to take oaths, appeared Cordra York, Sr., to me known personally and after being duly sworn, stated that the foregoing affidavit of two pages is true and correct to the best of his knowledge, information, and belief. I hereby certify that this document is the original affidavit of Cordra York, Sr.

In testimony whereof I have hereunto set my hand and affixed the seal of said Court, at office, in the City of Memphis, this 10th day of June, 1968.

[Signed] J. A. Blackwell, Clerk

AFFIDAVIT OF LIEUTENANT JAMES D. HAMBY

Now comes the affiant, after first being duly sworn, and states as follows:

That he is James D. Hamby, residing and domiciled at 2932 Armistead, Memphis, Shelby County, Tennessee, United States of America; that he is employed by the Memphis, Tennessee, Police Department, holding the rank of Lieutenant, and assigned to the Homicide Division of the aforesaid Police Department.

That on April 4, 1968, he was so employed and was on duty and acting in the aforesaid capacity; that he was assigned and participated in the investigation resulting from the slaying of Dr. Martin Luther King, Jr.; that as a part of his duties, pursuant to the investigation, he was present during the examination of the body of Dr. Martin Luther King, Jr., on April 4, 1968, at 2140 hours at John Gaston Hospital Morgue in Memphis, Shelby County, Tennessee.

That the medical examination was conducted by Dr. J. T. Francisco, medical examiner for Shelby County, Tennessee; that as a part of the examination Dr. Francisco removed from the body of Dr. Martin Luther King, Jr., one battered lead slug, and particularly marked with the autopsy number 252; that after the marking the said slug was placed in a manila envelope and given into custody of the affiant; that the affiant then proceeded to the Memphis, Tennessee, Police Department where the said slug was given into custody of Inspector N. E. Zachary, Inspector of Detectives of the Memphis, Tennessee, Police Department Homicide Division.

Affiant would further state that he has examined a certain lead slug this date now in the custody of the Clerk of the Criminal Court of Shelby County, Tennessee, and that it is the same slug which he has identified by the markings thereon as that removed from the body of Dr. Martin Luther King, Jr., in his presence at the morgue of the John Gaston Hospital, and subsequently given into the custody of Inspector Zachary.

That subsequently on April 5, 1968, the affiant, along with Special Agent Frank Johnson of the Memphis office of the Federal Bureau of Investigation, proceeded to the bathroom on the second floor of 422½ South Main Street, Memphis, Shelby County, Tennessee, a public rooming house, and Special Agent Johnson and the affiant physically removed the lower section of the wooden window sill of the bathroom, the window facing east overlooking the Lorraine Motel, that the aforesaid lower portion of the wooden window sill was of rough texture, and there was found in the approximate center of the sill a smooth, concave indentation which appeared to be of recent origin. That after the removal of the sill, same was taken into custody by the Federal Bureau of Investigation and sent to Washington, D. C., for criminal analysis by the Federal Bureau of Investigation laboratory, and that the same is retained in their custody.

Further affiant saith not.

[Signed] James D. Hamby
Lieutenant, Homicide Division
Memphis, Shelby County, Tennessee
Police Department
United States of America

STATE OF TENNESSEE
COUNTY OF SHELBY

Before me J. A. Blackwell, Clerk of the Criminal Courts of Shelby County, Tennessee, being an officer constituted to take oaths, appeared James D. Hamby, to me known personally and after being duly sworn, stated that the foregoing affidavit of two pages is true and correct to the best of his knowledge, information, and belief. I hereby certify that this document is the original affidavit of James D. Hamby.

In testimony whereof I have hereunto set my hand and affixed the seal of said Court, at office, in the City of Memphis, this 10th day of June, 1968.

[Signed] J. A. Blackwell, Clerk

AFFIDAVIT OF ROBERT G. JENSEN

I, Robert G. Jensen, being duly sworn depose and say:

1. I am 52 years of age and I reside at 1788 Bryn Mawr Circle, Germantown, Tennessee.

2. I am the Special Agent in Charge of the Memphis Division of the Federal Bureau of Investigation in Memphis, Tennessee. I am the senior officer in charge of the investigation in this area being conducted by the Federal Bureau of Investigation into the shooting of Dr. Martin Luther King, which took place on April 4, 1968.

3. On the evening of April 4, 1968, Inspector N. E. Zachary of the Memphis Police Department turned over to me numerous objects which he had personally recovered in connection with the shooting of Dr. Martin Luther King, Jr. Among the items which he turned over to me were a Remington Gamemaster Rifle, Model 760, Serial Number 461476, on which was mounted a Redfield telescopic sight. This rifle contained an empty shell casing which I removed. Among the other items furnished to me by Inspector Zachary were binoculars, trade name Banner by Bushnell, bearing Serial No. DQ408664; a gray paper bag bearing the firm name "York Arms Company"; a Peters cartridge box bearing Index Number 3033 and containing nine .30-06 caliber cartridges; and one Browning rifle box with markings indicating the box was for a .243 Winchester caliber rifle.

4. In addition to the above items, later in the evening of April 4, 1968, I received a bullet which had been removed from the body of the deceased Dr. Martin Luther King. This bullet was furnished by Inspector N. E. Zachary

to Special Agent Cyril F. Busch of the Federal Bureau of Investigation, who in turn delivered it to me.

5. All of the aforementioned items, including the empty shell casing which I removed from the rifle, were turned over by me to Special Agent Robert Fitzpatrich of the Federal Bureau of Investigation on the evening of April 4, 1968. I directed Special Agent Fitzpatrick to deliver all these items to the Laboratory of the Federal Bureau of Investigation in Washington, D. C.

[Signed] Robert G. Jensen
1788 Bryn Mawr Circle
Germantown, Tennessee

STATE OF TENNESSEE
COUNTY OF SHELBY

Before me J. A. Blackwell, Clerk of the Criminal Courts of Shelby County, Tennessee, being an officer constituted to take oaths, appeared Robert G. Jensen, to me known personally and after being duly sworn, stated that the foregoing affidavit of two pages is true and correct to the best of his knowledge, information, and belief. I hereby certify that this document is the original affidavit of Robert G. Jensen.

In testimony whereof I have hereunto set my hand and affixed the seal of said Court, at office, in the City of Memphis, this 10th day of June, 1968.

[Signed] J. A. Blackwell, Clerk

AFFIDAVIT OF JAMES H. LAUE

James H. Laue, being duly sworn, deposes and says:

1. I am 31 years old and reside in Alexandria, Virginia.

2. I am employed by the Community Relations Service, United States Department of Justice, Washington, D. C., as Acting Director, Program Evaluation and Development, and have been employed by the Community Relations Service since February 15, 1965.

3. I knew Dr. Martin Luther King, Jr. I had known him since 1960. I knew him both personally and professionally and saw him on numerous occasions. I also have been acquainted with his wife, Mrs. Coretta Scott King, for the past eight years.

4. On April 4, 1968, in pursuance of my official duties, I was in Memphis, Tennessee, to talk with Dr. King, and his staff about their activities in Memphis and Washington, D. C. I occupied Room 308 in the Lorraine Motel at 406 Mulberry Street in Memphis, Tennessee, on that day. Dr. King occupied Room 306 in that motel. I last saw him alive about 11:00 p.m., April 4, 1968.

5. At approximately 6:05 p.m. on April 4, 1968, while I was in my room at the Lorraine Motel, I heard a shot. I immediately went out of my room onto the balcony which surrounds the second floor of the motel. As I came out, I saw the body of a man lying on his back on the balcony about 20 feet to my right. I ran over to him and recognized at once this man as Dr. Martin Luther King, Jr. He was lying in a pool of blood, the bleeding coming from a large wound on the right side of his face, in the general area of the jaw and upper part of the neck.

Attached to this affidavit and designated as Exhibit I is a photograph. This photograph is a view from a building on the west side of Mulberry Street, looking generally in an easterly direction. This photograph is a fair and accurate representation of a substantial portion of the Lorraine Motel as it appeared on April 4, 1968, including the location of my room, Room 308, in the motel, and I have marked it with the letter "A". I have also placed an arrow above the door of the room where Dr. King stayed and have marked it with the letter "B". I have also circled the area where I saw Dr. King lying in a pool of blood in front of his room, as I have described in this affidavit, and I have marked that area with the letter "C".

6. Across Mulberry Street, west of the Lorraine Motel, is a row of buildings which fronts on the 400 block of South Main Street. Attached to this affidavit and designated as Exhibit II is a photograph. This photograph is taken from a balcony of the Lorraine Motel at or very near the spot where I saw Dr. King's body on April 4, 1968. This photograph looks in a generally westerly direction. The street seen in the photograph is Mulberry Street. The buildings across Mublerry Street front on South Main Street in the 400 block. This photograph is a fair and accurate representation as it looked on April 4, 1968 of the view of the back of the said buildings from the approximate point on the balcony of the Lorraine Motel where I found Dr. King lying that day.

7. I have been shown a copy of a survey of the area, appended to the affidavit of Robert V. Wenzler dated June 10, 1968, and a copy of which is appended hereto as Exhibit III. Based on my observation, this is a good representation of the relative locations of the Lorraine Motel and the buildings that front on the 400 block of South Main Street. I have placed an "X" at the point where I observed Dr. King's body on April 4, 1968, and a "Y" at the point described on the diagram (Exhibit III) as

67

"Point At Window From Which Shot Fired." From my observation on April 4, 1968, standing at point "X" and looking to point "Y", the view to the upper floor windows of that building at point "Y" is clear and unobstructed.

[Signed] James H. Laue

DISTRICT OF COLUMBIA

Subscribed and sworn to before me this 14th day of June, 1968.

I hereby certify that the attached three pages comprise the original affidavit of James H. Laue.

[Signed] Robert M. Stearns
Clerk, United States District Court
for the District of Columbia

Exhibit I to Affidavit of James H. Laue.

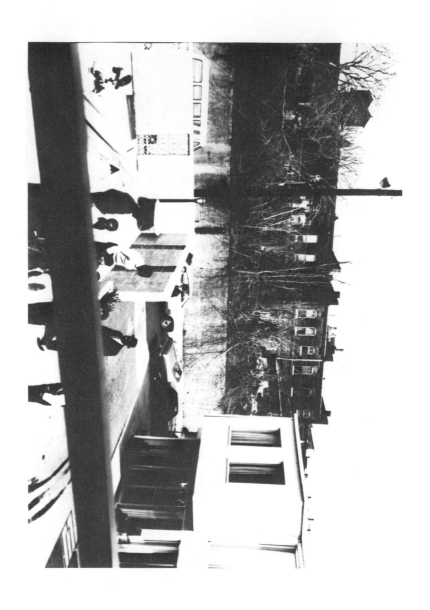

Exhibit II to Affidavit of James H. Laue.

70

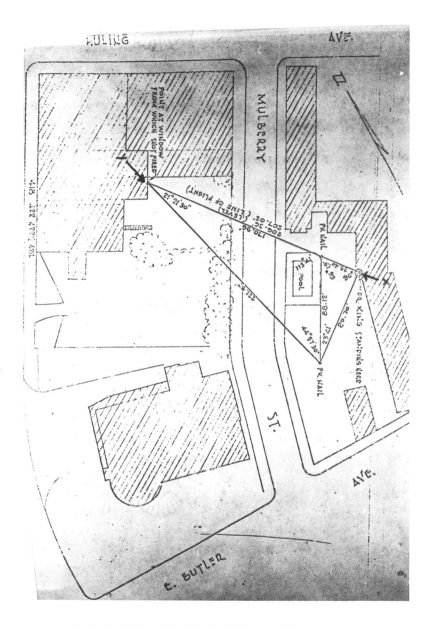

Exhibit III to Affidavit of James H. Lauc.

71

AFFIDAVIT OF CHARLES QUITMAN STEPHENS

I, Charles Quitman Stephens, being duly sworn, depose and say:

1. I am 46 years old and right now I have no fixed address. From March of 1967 until June of 1968, I lived at 422½ South Main Street, Memphis, Tennessee. On April 4, 1968, my common-law wife and I were living there in Apartment 6-B. The floor plan attached hereto and marked Exhibit I, the original of which I have signed, is a good likeness of the relationship of the rooms on the second floor, which was my floor.

2. Mrs. Bessie Brewer was the resident manager of the rooming house. At about 4:00 p.m., or a little later, on April 4, 1968, I thought I heard Mrs. Brewer's voice in the hall and I went out of my apartment to speak to her about the hot-water heater I had been working on. From the banister of the back stairs near my apartment door I saw her and a man standing in the hallway near the entrance to Room 5-B, which is just down the hall from my bedroom. I did not recognize the man with Mrs. Brewer and I assumed he was a new guest looking at the room. The man was looking into the room near the doorway and I got a glimpse at him from his left side. I have marked on the diagram a letter "A" where the man was standing, the letter "B" where Mrs. Brewer was standing, and the letter "X" where I was standing.

3. On April 24, 1968, I looked at FBI Wanted Flyer 442-A, and I identified the profile photograph on the left as looking very much like the man I saw looking at Room 5-B on the afternoon of April 4, 1968. A duplicate of that

72

Wanted Flyer, which I have signed, is attached and identified as Exhibit II. I now re-examine the photograph and reaffirm that identification. I also now examine another profile photograph, which appears to be a smaller copy of the one in the Flyer, and affirm that it looks very much like the man I saw looking at Room 5-B on the afternoon of April 4, 1968. This photograph is attached and identified as Exhibit III, and I have signed it. The pointed nose and chin are the principal features that stand out in my identification of the man pictured in Exhibit III as the man I saw with Mrs. Brewer looking into Room 5-B on April 4, 1968.

4. My wife and I spent the rest of the afternoon in our apartment. I am a disabled war veteran who has been treated for tuberculosis and spent most of my time in my bedroom. My wife was also ill and was at that time a bed patient.

5. After seeing the strange man with Mrs. Brewer, I heard someone in Room 5-B and assumed the man I had seen had rented the room next door. Several times that afternoon I heard footsteps in Room 5-B, and two or three times I heard footsteps leaving Room 5-B and going past my room and into the common bathroom at the end of the hall. The first couple of times the person from 5-B went to the bath he did not stay but a few minutes and once I heard the toilet flush. Each time I heard footsteps going back to Room 5-B. About the third time I heard footsteps from Room 5-B to the bathroom the person stayed what seemed like a long time. It seemed like a long time because while he was in there I wanted to use the toilet.

6. While this person was in there so long, Mr. Willie Anschutz, who lived in Room 4-B, knocked on my door and asked who the hell was staying in the bathroom so long. I opened my door and told him I didn't know, and he went back into his room.

7. Toward the end of the afternoon, sometime between 5:00 p.m. and 6:00 p.m., I was in my kitchen working on a small radio when I heard a shot. I have placed a double "XX" mark on the floor plan, Exhibit I, to show where I was when I heard the shot. I could tell that it came from the bathroom because it was very loud and the partition between my kitchen and the bathroom is thin plyboard.

8. I had not heard footsteps going back to Room 5-B between the time the person went in for so long and the time I heard the shot.

9. Right after the shot, I heard through a broken pane in my kitchen window a lot of voices yelling and hollering across the street from my building near the Lorraine Motel. I looked out my window toward the noise and I saw a lot of people milling around near the motel. Then I went to my door and opened it. I would say that about a minute, not more, passed between my hearing the shot and when I opened the door. First, I looked toward the bathroom and I saw that the door was open and it was empty. Then I went to the banister and looked the other way. When I did, I saw a man running near the end of the hallway. I have put an "O" mark on the floor plan, Exhibit I, to show about where he was when I saw him. He was carrying a bundle in his right hand. From what I could see, the bundle was at least three or four feet long and six or eight inches thick. The bundle appeared to be wrapped in what looked like newspaper. The man turned left toward the stairs when he reached the end of the hallway. Although I did not get a long look at him before he turned left, I think it was the same man I saw earlier with Mrs. Brewer looking at Room 5-B. The man running down the hall had on a dark suit, the same as the man I saw earlier.

10. Then I went back to my kitchen window. This time I saw a lot of people and policemen at the Lorraine Motel. A policeman near the embarkment behind my

building yelled at me to get away from the window, so I sat down in my bedroom.

[Signed] Charles Quitman Stephens

STATE OF TENNESSEE
COUNTY OF SHELBY

Sworn to and subscribed before me this 13th day of June 1968.

I hereby certify that this and the attached three pages and the attached documents identified as Exhibits I, II, and III comprise the original affidavit of Charles Quitman Stephens executed, sworn to, and subscribed before me this 13th day of June, 1968.

[Signed] W. Lloyd Johnson
Clerk, United States District Court
for the Western District of Tennessee

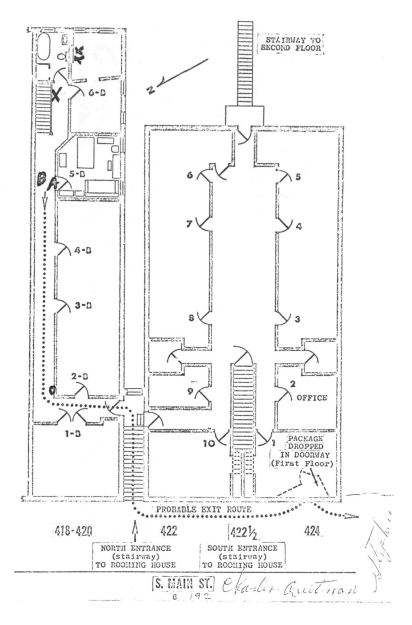

Exhibit I to Affidavit of Charles Quitman Stephens.

76

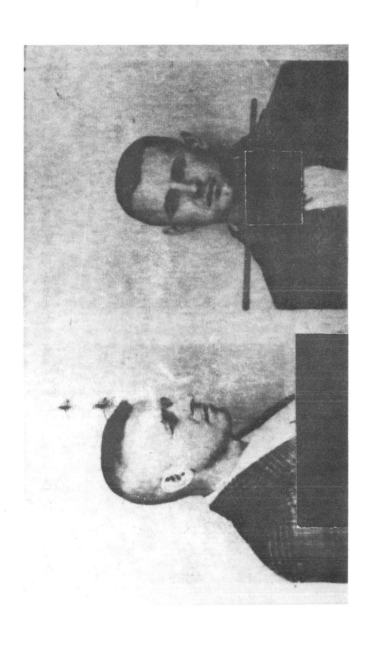

Exhibit III to Affidavit of Charles Quitman Stephens.

77

WANTED

BY THE **FBI**

CIVIL RIGHTS - CONSPIRACY
INTERSTATE FLIGHT - ROBBERY

JAMES EARL RAY

FBI No. 405,942 G

Photographs taken 1960

Photograph taken 1968
(eyes drawn by artist)

Aliases: Eric Starvo Galt, W. C. Herron, Harvey Lowmyer, James McBride, James O'Conner, James Walton, James Walyon, John Willard, "Jim."

Exhibit II to Affidavit of Charles Quitman Stephens.

78

DESCRIPTION

Age:	40, born March 10, 1928, at Quincy or Alton, Illinois (not supported by birth records)
Height:	5' 10"
Weight:	163 to 174 pounds
Build	Medium
Hair:	Brown, possibly cut short
Eyes:	Blue
Complexion:	Medium
Race:	White
Nationality:	American

Occupations: Baker, color matcher, laborer

Scars and Marks: Small scar on center of forehead and small scar on palm of right hand

Remarks: Noticeably protruding left ear; reportedly is a lone wolf; allegedly attended dance instruction school; has reportedly completed course in bartending.

Finger print Classification: 16 M 9 U OOO 12

M 4 W 1OI

CRIMINAL RECORD

Ray has been convicted of burglary, robbery, forging U. S. Postal Money Orders, armed robbery, and operating motor vehicle without owner's consent.

CAUTION

RAY IS SOUGHT IN CONNECTION WITH A MURDER WHEREIN THE VICTIM WAS SHOT. CONSIDER ARMED AND EXTREMELY DANGEROUS.

A Federal warrant was issued on April 17, 1968, at Birmingham, Alabama, charging Ray as Eric Starvo Galt with conspiring to interfere with a Constitutional Right of a citizen (Title 18, U. S. Code, Section 241). A Federal warrant was also issued on July 20, 1967, at Jefferson City, Missouri, charging Ray with Interstate Flight to Avoid Confinement for the crime of Robbery (Title 18, U. S. Code, Section 1073).

IF YOU HAVE ANY INFORMATION CONCERNING THIS PERSON, PLEASE NOTIFY ME OR CONTACT YOUR LOCAL FBI OFFICE. TELEPHONE NUMBERS AND ADDRESSES OF ALL FBI OFFICES LISTED ON BACK.

DIRECTOR
FEDERAL BUREAU OF INVESTIGATION
UNITED STATES DEPARTMENT OF JUSTICE
WASHINGTON, D. C. 20535
TELEPHONE, NATIONAL 8-7117

Wanted Flyer 442-A
April 19, 1968

EXHIBIT 11
TO THE AFFIDAVIT OF
CHARLES QUITMAN STEPHENS

79

AFFIDAVIT OF DONALD F. WOOD

I, Donald F. Wood, being duly sworn, depose and say:

1. I reside at 405 Lance Lane, Birmingham, Alabama and am employed by my father Robert E. Wood, Sr. at his store Aeromarine Supply Company, 5701 Airport Highway, Birmingham, Alabama as a salesman.

2. On Friday, March 29, 1968, in the early afternoon I observed Mr. U. L. Baker, also a salesman at the Aeromarine Supply Company, completing the sale of a rifle to an individual unknown to me. The purchaser had given his name as Harvey Lowmeyer. He purchased a Remington Model 700, caliber .243 Winchester with a Redfield scope mounted thereon, and 20 rounds of .243 ammunition.

3. Later that afternoon someone identifying himself as Lowmeyer called on the telephone and stated that he had had a conversation with his brother and had decided that he wished to exchange the rifle he had purchased for a Remington Model 760, 30.06 caliber. I agreed to make this exchange at additional cost.

4. At approximately 9:00 o'clock a.m. on Saturday, March 30, 1968 the same individual returned to the store with the gun he had previously purchased. I told him that I would change the scope from the caliber .243 rifle to the model 760, but that it would take me until approximately 3:00 o'clock in the afternoon.

5. He returned that afternoon and I gave him the Model 760 gun with the scope mounted on it. The Serial No. of the gun was 461476, and a copy of the sales invoice is attached to this affidavit as Exhibit I. I also exchanged the box of .243 caliber ammunition for a box of 30.06 ammunition. I did not charge him the additional amount

as anticipated because the base and rings used mounting the scope for the second gun were less expensive and made up the difference. The purchaser left the store carrying the gun in a cardboard box utilized by the Browning Manufacturing Company. This box was given to him because, with the scope mounted on it the rifle would not fit in the normal Remington box.

6. On April 16, 1968 I was visited by two agents of the Federal Bureau of Investigation and shown photographs of seven white males. After viewing the group of photographs which were identified to me only by number, and after careful consideration, I selected the photograph which had been marked No. 5 (attached to this affidavit as Exhibit II) as the man to whom the rifle was sold on March 29, 1968 and who returned it to me on March 30, 1968 in exchange for a Remington Model 760. At that time I advised the agents of the Federal Bureau of Investigation as follows: "I can't say exactly at this time, but I think this is the man. To the best of my memory I believe that this is the man that bought the gun".

7. Upon examining the photograph again today I reaffirm the statement I made on April 16, 1968, to the agents of the Federal Bureau of Investigation.

[Signed] Donald F. Wood

CITY OF BIRMINGHAM
STATE OF ALABAMA

Sworn to and subscribed before me this 10th day of June, 1968.

I hereby certify that this document is the original affidavit of Donald F. Wood.

[Signed] William E. Davis
Clerk, United States District Court
for the Northern District of Alabama

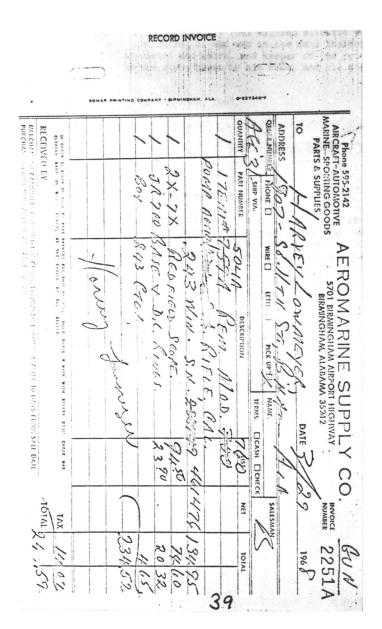

Exhibit I to Affidavit of Donald F. Wood.

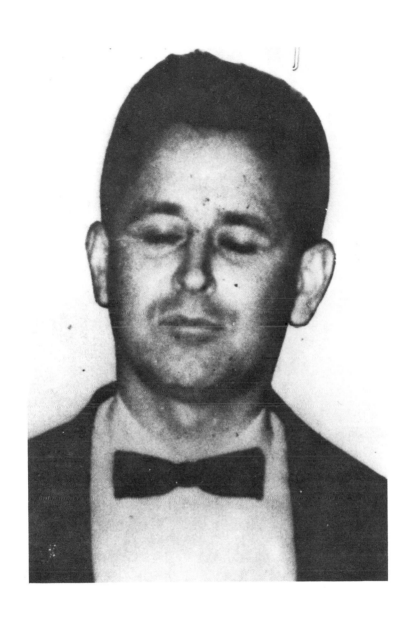

Exhibit II to Affidavit of Donald F. Wood.

AFFIDAVIT OF JOHN WEBSTER DE SHAZO

I, John Webster De Shazo, being duly sworn, depose and say:

1. I am twenty-five years old. I reside at 17 Montevallo Lane, Mountain Brook, Alabama, and am a frequent customer at the Aeromarine Supply Company, 5701 Airport Highway, Birmingham, Alabama. I am presently on a vacation trip in Los Angeles, California.

2. On March 29, 1968, I went to the Aeromarine Supply Company, arriving sometime around three o'clock p.m. It was my intention to purchase from Donald F. Wood a gun case for my rifle. Mr. Wood was absent from the store and I awaited his return.

3. About twenty minutes after I arrived, a man in a dark brown business suit came into the store. He looked at and handled several different weapons. He purchased a Remington Model 700, calibre .243 Winchester and a Redfield variable power telescopic sight and Redfield Jr. mounts.

4. After Donald F. Wood returned to the store, I purchased from him a gun case. Approximately forty-five minutes after the man in the brown suit entered the store, I departed. When I left the store, the man was still there waiting for the scope to be mounted and bore-sighted on the rifle. I had observed the man in the brown suit for a substantial portion of the time we were in the store together.

5. While in the store, I discussed with the man in the brown suit the gun he was purchasing. He stated that he was going deer hunting in Wisconsin with a brother or brother-in-law.

6. On April 16, 1968, I was visited by two agents of the Federal Bureau of Investigation who showed me seven photographs of seven different white males. From this group of photographs, which were identified to me only by number, I selected the photograph which had been marked number five on the back as the photograph of the man I observed on March 29, 1968, at the Aeromarine Supply Company in Birmingham and who I saw purchase a Remington Model 700, calibre .243 Winchester rifle and Redfield variable power telescopic sight. A copy of the photograph which I identified is attached to this affidavit as Exhibt I. I have initialed and dated the rear side of Exhibit I.

7. At the time of my identification of this photograph on April 16, 1968, and today, I believe that the man depicted in photograph Exhibit I is the man in the brown suit that I observed purchase a Remington Model 700, calibre .243 Winchester rifle and Redfield variable power telescopic sight at the Aeromarine Supply Company on March 29, 1968. I could be more positive of this identification if I saw this individual in person.

[Signed] John Webster De Shazo

UNITED STATES OF AMERICA
CENTRAL DISTRICT OF CALIFORNIA
COUNTY OF LOS ANGELES

Subscribed and sworn to before me this 13th day of June, 1968.

I hereby certify that the attached two pages comprise the original affidavit of John Webster De Shazo.

[Signed] John A. Childress
Clerk of the United States District Court
for the Central District of California

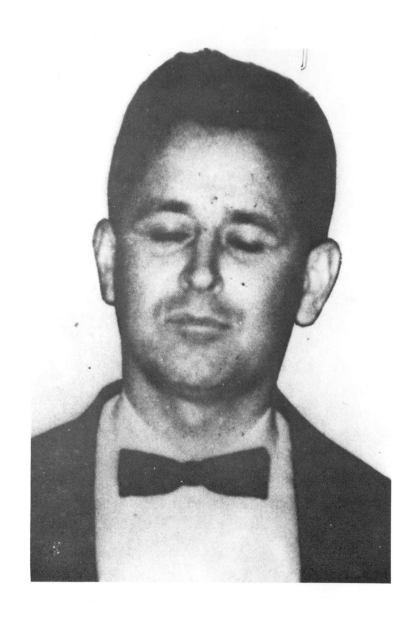

Exhibit I to Affidavit of John Webster De Shazo.

AFFIDAVIT OF ROBERT A. FRAZIER

Robert A. Frazier, being duly sworn, deposes and says:

1. I am 49 years old and I reside in Hillcrest Heights, Maryland.

2. I obtained a Bachelor of Science Degree from the University of Idaho in 1940. I have been a Special Agent of the Federal Bureau of Investigation since December 1942. I am Chief of the Firearms Unit of the Physics and Chemistry Section of the Federal Bureau of Investigation laboratory in Washington, D. C. I have been assigned to the Firearms Unit continuously since June 9, 1941. I received the specialized training program in firearms identification of approximately one year duration from the Federal Bureau of Investigation when I was initially assigned to the Firearms Unit. Since being assigned to this unit I have made thousands of comparisons of bullets and cartridge cases with the firearms for the purpose of determining whether a particular firearm fired a bullet or cartridge case. I have testified on numerous occasions in federal and state courts, as well as in military courts martial, as a firearms identification expert witness.

3. On April 5, 1968, at the Federal Bureau of Investigation Laboratory, I received certain items of evidence from Robert Fitzpatrick, Special Agent of the Federal Bureau of Investigation who had brought them by airplane from Memphis, Tennessee. These objects had been obtained in connection with the investigation of the shooting of Martin Luther King, Jr. on the previous day.

4. Among the items of evidence I received was a .30-06 Springfield caliber Remington rifle, Model 760, serial number 461476, with clip, and a Redfield telescopic sight, serial number A17350. I also received from Special Agent Fritzpatrick a .30 caliber metal-jacketed "soft-point" sporting type Remington-Peters cartridges and four

unfired .30-06 Springfield caliber U. S. military cartridges containing full metal-jacketed bullets.

5. I determined from microscopic examination that the expended .30 caliber metal-jacketed rifle bullet had been fired from a barrel rifled with six lands and grooves, right twist. As a result of my examination of the submitted rifle I determined that it produces general rifling impressions on fired bullets having the physical characteristics of those on the submitted bullet. I also determined that the submitted bullet was a 150-grain soft-point bullet identical to the bullets in the five Remington-Peters cartridges contained in the submitted Peters cartridge box.

6. Because of distortion due to mutilation and insufficient marks of value, I could draw no conclusion as to whether or not the submitted bullet was fired from the submitted rifle.

7. The .30-06 Springfield caliber Remington-Peters cartridge case was identified by me as having been fired in and extracted from the submitted rifle. This determination was based on a comparison of the microscopic markings of the firing pin, bolt face and extractor left on the cartridge case by the rifle. Based on physical characteristics, I determined that the fired bullet was of a kind that the manufacturer loads into the submitted cartridge case to produce cartridges similar to the Remington-Peters cartridges in the Peters cartridge box.

[Signed] Robert A. Frazier

DISTRICT OF COLUMBIA

Sworn to before me this 10th day of June, 1968.

I hereby Certify that the attached three pages comprise the original affidavit of Robert A. Frazier.

[Signed] Eleanor E. Jobe, Deputy Clerk
United States District Court for the District of Columbia

AFFIDAVIT OF GEORGE J. BONEBRAKE

George J. Bonebrake, being duly sworn, deposes and says:

1. I am a Fingerprint Examiner in the Federal Bureau of Investigation in Washington, D. C. I have held this position since October 1941. I have attended schools and other training classes conducted by the Federal Bureau of Investigation to qualify me for my position. During the time I have been a Fingerprint Examiner, I have made millions of fingerprint comparisons for identification purposes. I have testified as a fingerprint expert witness in numerous cases in federal and state courts as well as in military courts-martial with regard to my findings based on comparisons of fingerprints.

2. On April 5, 1968, at approximately 5:15 a.m., at the Federal Bureau of Investigation in Washington, D. C., I received certain objects of evidence from Special Agent Robert Fitzpatrick. These objects were identified to me as being part of the investigation into the shooting of Martin Luther King, Jr. in Memphis, Tennessee, on the previous day. Among the items delivered to me were a Remington Model 760 rifle, serial number 461476, with Redfield telescopic sight number A 17350, and a pair of 7 by 35 Bushnell binoculars, serial number DQ 408664. I examined each of these objects for latent fingerprints, and subsequently on April 5, 1968, I developed one latent fingerprint on the rifle, one latent fingerprint on the telescopic sight, and one latent fingerprint on the binoculars. These were the only latent prints on these objects which contained sufficient characteristic ridge detail to be of value for identification purposes.

3. On April 19, 1968, I compared each of the

afore-mentioned three latent prints with the known fingerprints of James Earl Ray obtained by officials of the Los Angeles Police Department, Los Angeles, California, on October 11, 1949. The fingerprint card made by the Los Angeles Police Department is contained in the official fingerprint files of the Federal Bureau of Investigation in Washington, D. C. From my comparison I formed the opinion that they were the fingerprints of the same man. I determined that the latent fingerprint on the Remington rifle and the latent fingerprint on the binoculars are identical to the left thumbprint of James Earl Ray, and that the latent fingerprint on the telescopic sight is identical to the right ring-fingerprint of James Earl Ray.

4. The official fingerprint files of the Federal Bureau of Investigation in Washington also contain the fingerprint record of James Earl Ray, taken in connection with his incarceration in the Missouri State Penitentiary on March 17, 1960, following the conviction of first degree robbery. I have compared the fingerprints of James Earl Ray taken in connection with his arrest on October 11, 1949, by the Los Angeles Police Department with the fingerprints taken in connection with the incarceration of James Earl Ray in the Missouri State Pentitentiary on March 17, 1960, and I have determined that these prints are of the same person.

5. Attached as Exhibit I is a photographic copy of the known prints of James Earl Ray, taken in connection with his arrest on October 11, 1949, by the Los Angeles, California Police Department. Attached as Exhibit II is a photographic copy of the known prints of James Earl Ray, taken on March 17, 1960, in connection with his incarceration in the Missouri State Penitentiary. Attached as Exhibits III, IV and V are three photographs, each depicting one of the afore-mentioned three latent fingerprints developed by me respectively on the rifle, the telescopic sight, and the binoculars.

6. I am also an Assistant Custodian of the fingerprint

records of the Identification Division of the Federal Bureau of Investigation. As such, I am familiar with the contents of those records and am authorized to have copies made of those records and to certify as to their authenticity.

7. The fingerprint card attached as Exhibit II on Form FD-249, is a true copy of the original record in my custody and was prepared under my supervision. The original was received by the Federal Bureau of Investigation from the Warden of the State Penitentiary at Jefferson City, Missouri, on April 4, 1960 and contains the photograph (profile and front view), fingerprints, and signature of James Earl Ray, an inmate of the Penitentiary then serving a 20-year sentence.

[Signed] George J. Bonebrake

DISTRICT OF COLUMBIA

Sworn to me this 10th day of June, 1968.

I hereby certify that the attached three pages comprise the original affidavit of George J. Bonebrake.

[Signed] Eleanor E. Jobe
Deputy Clerk, United States District Court
for the District of Columbia

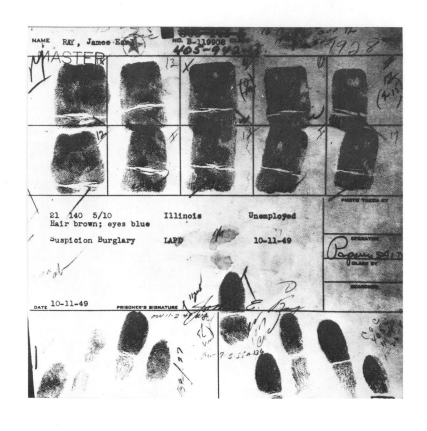

Exhibit I to Affidavit of George J. Bonebrake.

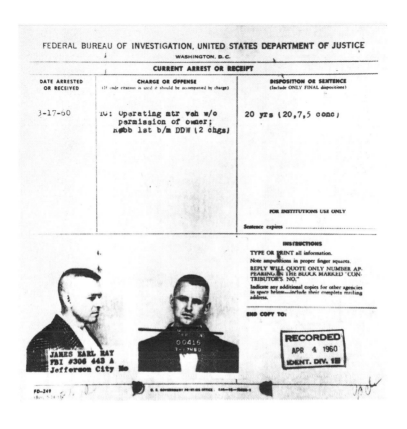

FEDERAL BUREAU OF INVESTIGATION, UNITED STATES DEPARTMENT OF JUSTICE

WASHINGTON, D.C.

CURRENT ARREST OR RECEIPT

DATE ARRESTED OR RECEIVED	CHARGE OR OFFENSE (If code citation is used it should be accompanied by charge)	DISPOSITION OR SENTENCE (Include ONLY FINAL dispositions)
3-17-60	1C: Operating mtr veh w/o permission of owner; Robb 1st b/m DDW (2 chgs)	20 yrs (20,7,5 conc)

FOR INSTITUTIONS USE ONLY

Sentence expires ....

INSTRUCTIONS

TYPE OR PRINT all information.

Note amputations in proper finger squares.

REPLY WILL QUOTE ONLY NUMBER APPEARING IN THE BLOCK MARKED "CONTRIBUTOR'S NO."

Indicate any additional copies for other agencies in space below—include their complete mailing address.

END COPY TO:

RECORDED
APR 4 1960
IDENT. DIV. 18

JAMES EARL RAY
FBI #308 443 A
Jefferson City Mo

FD-249

Exhibit II (front) to Affidavit of George J. Bonebrake.

93

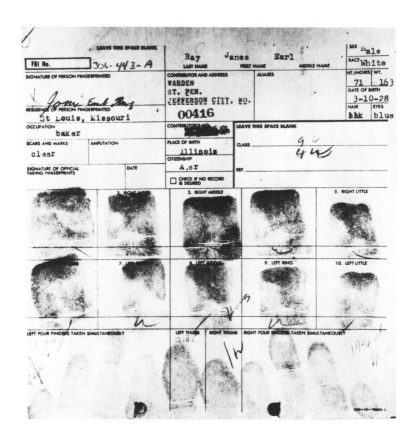

Exhibit II (back) to Affidavit of George J. Bonebrake.

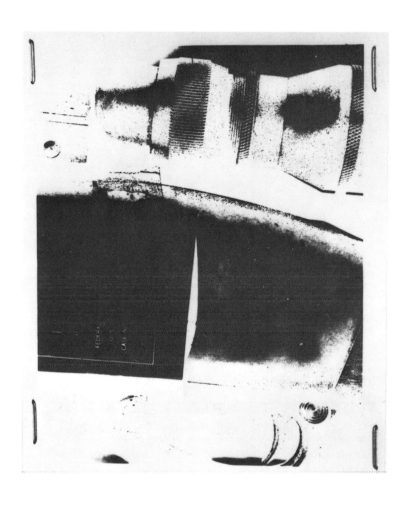

Exhibit III to Affidavit of George J. Bonebrake.

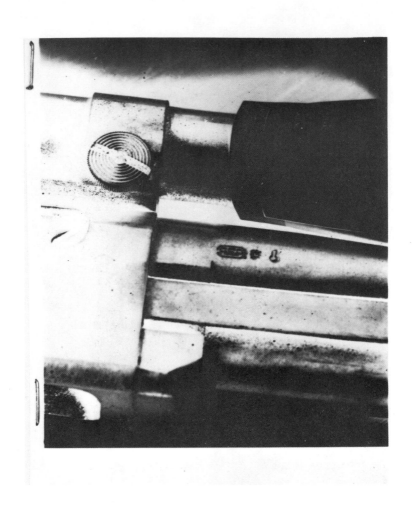

Exhibit IV to Affidavit of George J. Bonebrake.

Exhibit V to Affidavit of George J. Bonebrake.

AFFIDAVIT OF LYNDAL L. SHANEYFELT

Lyndal L. Shaneyfelt, being duly sworn, deposes and says:

1. I am a Special Agent of the Federal Bureau of Investigation, and am assigned to the Laboratory of the Federal Bureau of Investigation at its Headquarters Office in Washington, D. C. I have been employed by the Federal Bureau of Investigation continuously since 1940, except for almost one year of army service in 1945. From 1940 until 1951 I did photographic work. In 1951 I became a Special Agent and was assigned as a field investigator to the Detroit Field Office. Since 1952 I have been employed continuously and exclusively in examining questioned documents and photographic evidence. I have received training in this specialized field in the Laboratory, attending lectures, reading the recommended literature on the subject, and conducting experiments, as well as working initially as an apprentice under an experienced examiner. During the course of my career I have examined thousands of photographs for the purposes of comparison, including comparisons to establish the identification of individuals.

2. I have examined the photograph attached as Exhibit II to the affidavit of Donald F. Wood, a copy of which photograph also appears as Exhibit I attached to this affidavit, and compared it with the photographs attached as Exhibit II to the affidavit of George J. Bonebrake, a copy of which photographs also appear as Exhibit II attached to this affidavit, and have concluded from my examination which involved a comparison of the front view of the individual depicted in the attachment to the Wood affidavit that these two photographs depict the same individual.

3. I have based my conclusion on a comparison of all of the facial characteristics in these photographs, including the contour of the ears, nose, mouth, areas surrounding the eyes, and the significant wrinkles and lines appearing in the face.

[Signed] Lyndal L. Shaneyfelt

DISTRICT OF COLUMBIA

Subscribed and sworn to before me this 11th day of June, 1968.

I hereby certify that the attached two pages comprise the original affidavit of Lyndal L. Shaneyfelt.

[Signed] Robert M. Stearns
Clerk, United States District Court
for the District of Columbia

CERTIFICATION

I, George L. Hart, Jr., Judge, United States District Court for the District of Columbia, do hereby certify that Robert M. Stearns, whose name and signature appear on the attached affidavit, is and was at the date thereof Clerk of said Court, duly appointed and sworn, and is authorized to administer an oath for general purposes.

This the 11th day of June, 1968.

[Signed] George L. Hart, Jr.
Judge, United States District Court
for the District of Columbia

United States
Department of Justice

685403-2

Washington, D.C., _____June 11_____, 19 68

o whom these presents shall come, Greeting:

ify That _____George L. Hart, Jr._____ whose name is signed to
anying paper , is now, and was at the time of signing the same,

_____United States District Court for the District of Columbia_____

_____ duly commissioned and qualified.

ness, whereof, I, _____Ramsey Clark_____

Attorney General of the United States, have
hereunto caused the Seal of the Department
of Justice to be affixed and my name to be
attested by the ~~Assistant Attorney General for Administration~~
~~Assistant~~ of the said Department on the day
and year first above written.

Ramsey Clark

Attorney General.

By _____

Assistant Attorney General for Administration

100

United States of America

DEPARTMENT OF STATE

to whom these presents shall come, Greeting:

ertify That the document hereunto annexed is under the seal

Department of Justice of the United States of America,

is entitled to full faith and credit.

In testimony whereof, I, _____

Secretary of State, have hereunto caused the seal of the Department of State to be affixed and my name subscribed by the Authentication Officer of the said Department, at the city of Washington, in the District of Columbia, this _____

day of _____, 19____ .

_____
Secretary of State.

By _____
Authentication Officer, Department of State.

U.S. GOVERNMENT PRINTING OFFICE   16—80049-7

Issued pursuant to RS
5 USC 158; Sec. 1 of A
62 St. 466, 78 USC 177
May 26, 1949, 63 St. 11
Secs. 104 and 332 of Ac
66 St. 174 and 253, 8 U
5 USC 140.

101

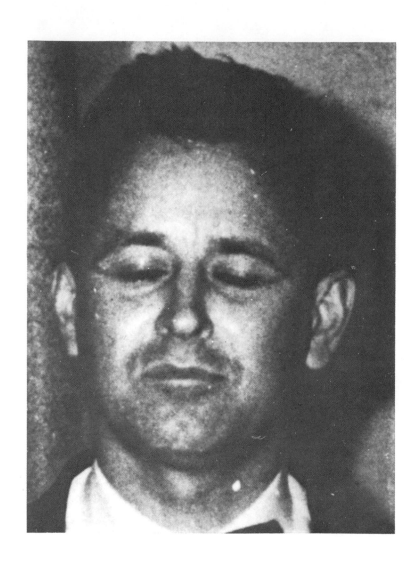

Exhibit I to Affidavit of Lyndal L. Shaneyfelt.

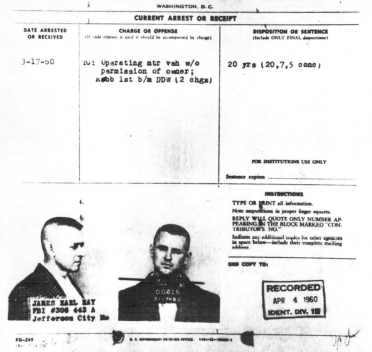

FEDERAL BUREAU OF INVESTIGATION, UNITED STATES DEPARTMENT OF JUSTICE

WASHINGTON, D. C.

CURRENT ARREST OR RECEIPT

DATE ARRESTED OR RECEIVED	CHARGE OR OFFENSE (If code citation is used it should be accompanied by charge)	DISPOSITION OR SENTENCE (Include ONLY FINAL dispositions)
3-17-60	10: Operating mtr veh w/o permission of owner; Robb 1st b/m DDW (2 chgs)	20 yrs (20,7,5 conc)
		FOR INSTITUTIONS USE ONLY Sentence expires ....

INSTRUCTIONS

TYPE OR PRINT all information.

Note amputations in proper finger squares.

REPLY WILL QUOTE ONLY NUMBER APPEARING IN THE BLOCK MARKED "CONTRIBUTOR'S NO."

Indicate any additional copies for other agencies in space below—include their complete mailing address.

SEND COPY TO:

RECORDED
APR 4 1960
IDENT. DIV. 18

JAMES EARL RAY
FBI #306 443 A
Jefferson City Mo

00416
3-17-60

FD-249
(Rev. 5-24-57)

U. S. GOVERNMENT PRINTING OFFICE : 249—16—72650-1

Exhibit II to Affidavit of Lyndal L. Shaneyfelt.

103

AFFIDAVIT OF TOMAS REYES LAU

I, Tomas Reyes Lau, being duly sworn, depose and say:

1. I am forty-four years old. I am the Director of the International School of Bartending located at 341 South Alvarado Street, Los Angeles, California, formerly located until April 15, 1968, at 2125 Sunset Boulevard, Los Angeles, California. I have been Director of this School since May, 1965. In that capacity, I am familiar with and have in my custody the records of the International School of Bartending which are kept in the ordinary course of business.

2. A man representing himself as Eric S. Galt attended the International School of Bartending from January 19, 1968, through March 2, 1968. I have checked with the dates of his attendance on my records. During the time that Mr. Galt was enrolled at the School, I would see him almost every working day. I was Mr. Galt's instructor for all classes.

3. On March 2, 1968, the man I knew as Eric S. Galt graduated from the International School of Bartending. A graduation photograph was taken at that event. Attached to this affidavit and designated as Exhibit I is a true copy of that photograph which bears my initials and this date on the reverse side. Looking at the photograph designated as Exhibit I, I am the man on the left, the man standing by my side is Eric S. Galt. This photograph represents a good likeness of the Mr. Galt who attended the International School of Bartending. On April 15, 1968, I gave the original photograph and the negative from which it was prepared to Theodore J. A'Hearn, Special Agent of the Federal Bureau of Investigation.

4. Attached to this affidavit and designated as Exhibit II is an enlarged black and white reproduction of the same photograph designated as Exhibit I. I have initialed and dated the rear side of Exhibit II. Again, in looking at photograph Exhibit II, I am the man on the left, the man standing by my side is Eric S. Galt. This photograph represents a good likeness of the Mr. Galt who attended the International School of Bartending. The document held by Mr. Galt is the graduation certificate bearing his name which I presented to him on March 2, 1968.

5. Attached to this affidavit and designated as Exhibit III is a photograph of the man I knew as Eric S. Galt. I have initialed and dated the rear side of this exhibit. This represents a good likeness of Mr. Galt.

6. On January 19, 1968, the man representing himself to be Eric S. Galt made application in person to me for admission to the International School of Bartending. I saw Eric S. Galt fill out and sign in his own handwriting the Application For School Admission. A true copy of this application, which bears my initials and this date on the reverse side, is attached to this affidavit and designated as Exhibit IV. I gave the original of the application to Special Agent A'Hearn on April 15, 1968.

7. At a time subsequent to Mr. Galt's enrollment at the International School of Bartending, Mr. Galt advised me of a change in his residence address. I modified the Application For School Admission form by striking the words "1535 North Serrano" and the telephone number "469-8096," and adding "5533 Hollywood Boulevard" and the telephone number "464-1131."

8. On January 19, 1968, in connection with his application for admission to the International School of Bartending, Eric S. Galt signed in my presence an Installment Note in the amount of One Hundred Twenty-five Dollars ($125.00) payable to the International School of Bartending for the six-week bartending course. A true copy of said Installment Note, which bears my initials and

this date on the reverse side, is attached to this affidavit and designated as Exhibit V. I gave the original of this Installment Note to Special Agent A'Hearn on April 15, 1968.

[Signed] Tomas Reyes Lau

UNITED STATES OF AMERICA
CENTRAL DISTRICT OF CALIFORNIA
COUNTY OF LOS ANGELES

Subscribed and sworn to before me this 13th day of June, 1968.

I hereby certify that the attached three pages comprise the original affidavit of Tomas Reyes Lau.

[Signed] John A. Childress
Clerk of the United States District Court
for the Central District of California

Exhibits I and II to Affidavit of Tomas Reyes Lau.

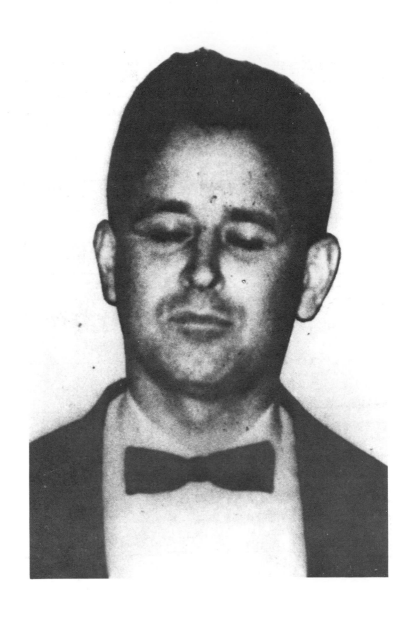

Exhibit III to Affidavit of Tomas Reyes Lau.

APPLICATION FOR EMPLOYMENT   Date. 1-19-68

NAME IN FULL (PRINT). _____   SOCIAL SECURITY REG. NO.

Address. 18357 - Street   Phone No. 464-9694   SELECTIVE SERVICE CLASSIFICATION. 3-A
6526 Hollywood Blvd   464-1131
Birthday: Month 7 Day 30 Year 31

Are you a citizen of the United States? YES

If not, do you intend to become a citizen?

Married, Divorced, or Single SINGLE   Number of Children NONE

List below the Names and Addresses of your former employers:

Name	Address	FROM (Date)	TO (Date)	Salary	Why did you leave?
R. WILLER	251-S-FIGEROA			500 00	

Give Names and Addresses of three character references: (Do not name Relatives or former Employers here.)

Name	Address
Marie Denino	5533 Hollywood Bl. Hollywood
Gene Steen	5666 Franklin, Hollywood, Calif
Emily Denino	5666 Franklin, Hollywood, Calif

Education: (State schooling you have had) High School

What work do you do best?   Weight 175
What other work are you fitted for?   Height 5-10
What physical defects have you? NONE

I hereby grant permission to investigate any of the information included in this application.
Signature of Applicant Eric D. Galt

APPLICANT: DO NOT WRITE BELOW THIS LINE

References checked by   Initial rate   per   Date started   DEPT.
Entered on Payroll   Date   By
Approved

BCK CAT FORM 415

Exhibit IV to Affidavit of Tomas Reyes Lau.

109

INSTALLMENT NOTE — INTEREST EXTRA

$ 125.00   L.A.,   California,   Jan. 19   , 19 63 .

In installments as herein stated, for value received, __I__ promise to pay to _____

INTERNATIONAL SCHOOL OF BARTENDING _____ or order,

at _____

the sum of ONE HUNDRED TWENTYFIVE NO/00--- _____ DOLLARS

with interest from _____ on unpaid principal at the rate of

_____ per cent per annum, payable _____

_____ ; principal payable in installments of

_____ Dollars

or more on the _____ day of each _____ month, beginning

on the _____ day of _____

$125.00 Onehundred tweentyfive no/00 dollars for six weeks Bartending
Course. Cash payment and there are absolutely no refunds.

_____ and continuing until said principal and interest have been paid.

Should interest not be so paid it shall thereafter bear like interest as the principal. Should default be made in payment
of any installment of principal or interest when due the whole sum of principal and interest shall become immediately due at
the option of the holder of this note. Principal and interest payable in lawful money of the United States. If action be in-
stituted on this note __I__ promise to pay such sum as the Court may fix as attorney's fees.

Eric S. Galt

Tomás Reyes Lau

85179

Exhibit V to Affidavit of Tomas Reyes Lau.

110

AFFIDAVIT OF THEODORE J. A'HEARN

I, Theodore J. A'Hearn, being duly sworn, depose and say:

1. I am forty-two years of age and I reside in LaCanada, California.

2. I am a Special Agent of the Federal Bureau of Investigation assigned to the Los Angeles Division.

I have examined the affidavit of Tomas Reyes Lau dated June 13, 1968, and the exhibits attached to it.

On April 15, 1968, Mr. Tomas Reyes Lau turned over to me at Los Angeles, California, the originals of a photograph and two documents, copies of which are appended to his affidavit and marked as Exhibits I, IV and V. On April 15, 1968, I mailed these documents by registered mail to the Director, Federal Bureau of Investigation, Washington, D. C., to the attention of the FBI Laboratory.

[Signed] Theodore J. A'Hearn

UNITED STATES OF AMERICA
CENTRAL DISTRICT OF CALIFORNIA
COUNTY OF LOS ANGELES

Subscribed and sworn to before me this 13th day of June, 1968.

I hereby certify that the attached one page comprises the original affidavit of Theodore J. A'Hearn.

[Signed] John A. Childress
Clerk of the United States District Court
for the Central District of California

AFFIDAVIT OF HENRIETTA HAGEMASTER

I, Henrietta Hagemaster, being duly sworn, depose and say:

1. I am 37 years old. I have been employed for about 9 years as a desk clerk at the New Rebel Motor Hotel, 3466 Lamar Avenue, Memphis, Tennessee, and was so employed on April 3, 1968. I was on duty there from 2:00 p.m. to 10:00 p.m. on that day.

2. Among my duties at the motel I see that each arriving guest renting a room at the motel signs a registration card and furnishes the information requested on the card. After the guest fills in the information, I insert the room number, daily rate, arrival date, number in the party and time of the guest's registration. It is my practice to turn around to look at the clock behind the desk to note the time which I then record on the card in the box marked "Dept. Date." I do this because our practice is to allow guests fifteen minutes to inspect their rooms and to cancel their registration without charge if the room is not satisfactory. I then place the registration card in a cabinet-type card rack which is mounted on the wall directly behind the registration desk. We keep each guest's card in the rack until he checks out, and then it is transferred to the card file which is kept in the office upstairs by Miss Kelly, the manager of the motel.

3. About a week after Dr. King was killed I was shown one of our registration cards by Mr. John W. Bauer who identified himself to me as a Special Agent of the Federal Bureau of Investigation. A copy of that registration card (front and back) is attached hereto and designated as

Exhibit I. I recognize that card as one filled out and signed in my presence by the person who registered as Eric S. Galt, 2608 Highland Avenue, Birmingham, Alabama, on April 3, 1968, at 7:15 p.m. The room number (34), rate ($6.24), date (4-3-68), time (7:15 p.m.), number in party (1), and clerk's initials (H H) were all entered by me and are in my handwriting. Based on our usual practice, the rest of the front of the card was filled out by the guest (name, address, car license, state, and make of car), and the handwriting in those spaces on the card shown to me by Mr. Bauer, a copy of which is attached, is not mine.

[Signed] Henrietta Hagemaster

STATE OF TENNESSEE
COUNTY OF SHELBY

I hereby certify that this and the attached page and the attached document identified as Exhibit I comprise the original affidavit of Henrietta Hagemaster executed, sworn to, and subscribed before me this 14th day of June, 1968.

[Signed] W. Lloyd Johnson
Clerk, United States District Court
for the Western District of Tennessee

AFFIDAVIT OF ANNA CHRISTINE KELLY

I, Anna Christine Kelly, being duly sworn, depose and say:

1. I am 56 years old. I am the manager of Vic Dupratt's New Rebel Motor Hotel, which is located at 3466 Lamar Avenue, Memphis, Tennessee, and I keep its business records. I have been the manager of the motel since 1958 and as such I was, on April 3-4, 1968, the keeper of the records.

2. Among the business records in my custody are the original registration cards of the guests who stay at the motel. I know it is the standard operating practice for the desk clerks to require each guest renting a room at the motel to sign at the time of registration a registration card in his own handwriting and to fill in his name, address and the identity of the firm he represents, if any. Some guests also fill in the registration card spaces for "car license," "make of car," and "State" near the bottom of the front of the card. Our clerks verify the information about each car and make any necessary corrections or fill in any information that the guest has omitted. Our clerks regularly fill in the blanks labeled "Room," "Rate," "Dept. Date," "Arr. Date," "No. in Party," and "Clerk." Most of our clerks insert the arrival times of guests in the blank "Dept. Date." I know that Mrs. Hagemaster follows this practice. The backs of the cards are filled out by our clerks only. The original registration cards are turned over to me in the regular course of business and are maintained by me as part of the business records of the motel.

3. Among the registration cards maintained by me in the regular course of business was a card reflecting the

114

registration of one Eric S. Galt at the motel on April 3, 1968. On April 9, 1968, at the request of Special Agent Robert G. Jensen, of the Federal Bureau of Investigation, who had called at the motel, I made available to the Special Agents my file of registration cards. In a part of my office they went through the file and found this card of Mr. Galt. I was present during the entire time the agents were looking through my file. On April 9, 1968, I gave the registration card to Special Agent Robert G. Jensen of the Federal Bureau of Investigation, and received from him a receipt to that effect which I keep in my card file at the place where the original was located. Attached hereto and designated as Exhibit I is a true copy (front and back) of that registration card.

4. The registration card reflects that Eric S. Galt was charged for one day's lodging and departed on April 4, 1968. I infer from the established practice of the motel that he left by the checkout time, which is 1:00 p.m; otherwise, his registration card would have reflected a charge for two days' lodging instead of only one day.

5. I am familiar with the handwriting of Mrs. Henrietta Hagemaster, the desk clerk who was on duty from 2:00 p.m. on April 3, 1968, until 10:00 p.m. on that date. I have examined the registration card of Eric S. Galt. Looking at the card, I can say that the only handwriting on the front by Mrs. Hagemaster is in the spaces marked "Room," "Rate," "Arr. Date," "Dept. Date," "No. in Party," and "Clerk."

[Signed] Anna Christine Kelly

STATE OF TENNESSEE
COUNTY OF SHELBY

I hereby certify that this and the attached two pages and

the attached document identified as Exhibit I comprise the original affidavit of Anna Christine Kelly executed, sworn to, and subscribed before me this 13th day of June, 1968.

[Signed] W. Lloyd Johnson
Clerk, United States District Court
for the Western District of Tennessee

AFFIDAVIT OF ROBERT G. JENSEN

Robert G. Jensen, being duly sworn, deposes and says:

1. I am 52 years of age and I reside at 1788 Bryn Mawr Circle, Germantown, Tennessee.

2. I am the Special Agent in Charge of the Memphis Division of the Federal Bureau of Investigation in Memphis, Tennessee. I am the senior officer in charge of the investigation in this area being conducted by the Federal Bureau of Investigation into the shooting of Dr. Martin Luther King, Jr., which took place on April 4, 1968.

3. On April 9, 1968, Miss Anna Christine Kelly, manager of Vic Dupratt's New Rebel Motor Hotel, 3466 Lamar Avenue, Memphis, Tennessee, turned over to me the original registration card reflecting the registration of one Eric S. Galt at the Motor Hotel on April 3, 1968. Attached hereto and designated as Exhibit I is a true copy (front and back) of that registration card. On April 9, 1968, I forwarded the original registration card to the Federal Bureau of Investigation Laboratory, Washington, D. C., for a handwriting analysis.

[Signed] Robert G. Jensen

STATE OF TENNESSEE
COUNTY OF SHELBY

I hereby certify that this page and the attached document identified as Exhibit I comprise the original affidavit of

117

Robert G. Jensen executed, sworn to, and subscribed before me this 14th day of June, 1968.

[Signed] W. Lloyd Johnson
Clerk, United States District Court
for the Western District of Tennessee

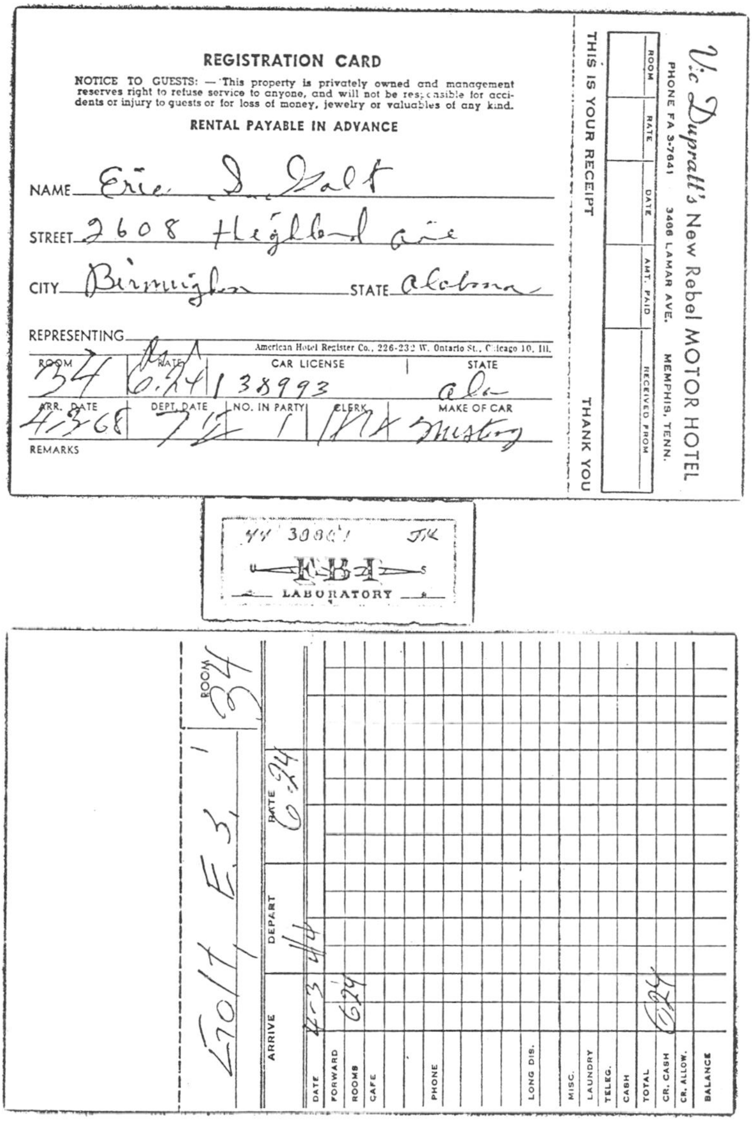

Exhibit I (front and back) to Affidavits of Henrietta Hagemaster, Anna Christine Kelly, and Robert G. Jensen

119

AFFIDAVIT OF JAMES H. MORTIMER

James H. Mortimer, being duly sworn, deposes and says:

1. I am 42 years old and reside in Springfield, Virginia. I attended Miami University at Oxford, Ohio and the University of South Carolina and received a Bachelor of Science degree at the latter in 1945. I also attended the University of Cincinnati.

2. I am a Special Agent of the Federal Bureau of Investigation, and am assigned to the Laboratory of the Federal Bureau of Investigation at its Headquarters Office in Washington, D. C. I have been employed by the Federal Bureau of Investigation continuously since July 21, 1952, when I entered on duty as a Special Agent. After an initial training period of sixteen weeks at the Washington, D. C. Headquarters Office, I was assigned to the Pittsburgh, Pennsylvania Division for a period of eighteen months and then was transferred to the Washington, D. C. Field Office, where I remained until March 16, 1959, when I was assigned to the Laboratory. I have been employed there since then exclusively and full-time as an examiner of questioned documents. I received extensive training in this highly specialized field, working originally as an apprentice under an experienced examiner for a period of three years. I attended lectures delivered by experts in this field and read the extensive literature of the subject.

3. As an examiner of questioned documents, I have examined and compared numerous written, typed and printed instruments for the purposes of determining questions of identity, authenticity, and the like. I have examined and compared samples of handwriting in thou-

120

sands of instances, and have testified as a handwriting expert in numerous trials in the federal and state courts.

4. On April 10, 1968, in the due course of business I received a sealed envelope which had been sent by registered mail from the Memphis Division of the Federal Bureau of Investigation. I opened the envelope and found therein a Registration Card labeled for the Vic Dupratt's New Rebel Motor Hotel, bearing the written signature "Eric S. Galt." A photographic copy of the face of the Registration Card, which is a true and faithful reproduction of the original, is attached hereto and designated as Exhibit I. A photographic copy of the back of the card, which is a true and faithful reproduction of the original, is attached hereto as Exhibit II.

5. On April 22, 1968, in the due course of business, I received a sealed envelope which had been sent by registered mail from the Los Angeles Division of the Federal Bureau of Investigation. I opened the envelope and found therein, among other items, two original documents. One was a printed form headed "APPLICATION FOR SCHOOL ADM." bearing at the top and bottom the handwritten signature "Eric S. Galt." A photographic copy of that document, which is a true and faithful reproduction of the original, is attached hereto as Exhibit III. The other document was a printed form headed "INSTALL-MENT NOTE—INTEREST EXTRA," bearing at the bottom the typewritten and handwritten signatures, "Eric S. Galt" and "Tomas Reyes Lau." A photographic copy of that document, which is a true and faithful reproduction of the original, is attached hereto as Exhibit IV.

6. I have compared the handwritten signature "Eric S. Galt" on the Registration Card of the New Rebel Motel in Memphis, Tennessee dated April 3, 1968 (a copy of which is attached as Exhibit I) with the two handwritten signatures "Eric S. Galt" on the application form (a copy of which is attached as Exhibit III) and with the

handwritten signature "Eric S. Galt" on the installment note (a copy of which is attached as Exhibit IV). As a result of my comparison, it is my opinion that all four of the aforesaid handwritten signatures "Eric S. Galt" were written by the same person.

[Signed] James H. Mortimer

DISTRICT OF COLUMBIA

Subscribed and sworn to before me this 14th day of June, 1968.

I hereby certify that the attached three pages comprise the original affidavit of James H. Mortimer.

[Signed] Robert M. Stearns
Clerk, United States District Court
for the District of Columbia

Vic Dupratt's New Rebel MOTOR HOTEL

PHONE FA 3-7641   3466 LAMAR AVE.   MEMPHIS, TENN.

ROOM	RATE	DATE	AMT. PAID	RECEIVED FROM

THIS IS YOUR RECEIPT   **THANK YOU**

REGISTRATION CARD

NOTICE TO GUESTS: —This property is privately owned and management reserves right to refuse service to anyone, and will not be responsible for accidents or injury to guests or for loss of money, jewelry or valuables of any kind.

RENTAL PAYABLE IN ADVANCE

NAME _Eric S. Galt_

STREET _2608 Highland Ave_

CITY _Birmingham_ STATE _Alabama_

REPRESENTING ____

American Hotel Register Co., 226-232 W. Ontario St., Chicago 10, Ill.

| DATE | CAR LICENSE | STATE |
| | _38993_ | _Ala._ |

ROOM _34_

DEPT. DATE _____ NO. IN PARTY _1_ CLERK ____ MAKE OF CAR _Mustang_

ARR. DATE _4/13/68_

REMARKS

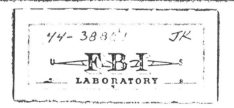

Exhibit I to Affidavit of James H. Mortimer.

123

Exhibit II to Affidavit of James H. Mortimer.

APPLICATION FOR EMPLOYMENT   Date... 1-19-68

NAME IN FULL (PRINT)... Eric S. Galt

SOCIAL SECURITY REG. NO. ...

Address... 1535 N. Serrano ... Phone No... 464-9696 ... SELECTIVE SERVICE CLASSIFICATION... 3-A

6525 Hollywood Blvd

Age 36... Birthday: Month 7 Day 20 Year 31   464-1131

Are you a citizen of the United States?... YES

If not, do you intend to become a citizen?...

Married, Divorced, or Single... SINGLE ... Number of Children... NONE

Give below the Names and Addresses of your former employers:

Name	Address	FROM (Date)	TO (Date)	Salary	Why did you leave?
Galt	Free				
R. WILLER	251 - S - FIGEROA			5000	

Give Names and Addresses of three character references: (Do not name Relatives or former Employers here.)

Name	Address
Carl Penamac	5533 Hollywood B.C. Hollywood
Pete Steen	5666 Franklin, Hollywood calif
Holly Denning	5666 Franklin, Hollywood, calif

Education: (State schooling you have had)... High School

What work do you do best?...

What other work are you fitted for?... Weight... 175

What physical defects have you? NONE ... Height... 5-10

I hereby grant permission to investigate any of the information included in this application.

Signature of Applicant... Eric S. Galt

APPLICANT: DO NOT WRITE BELOW THIS LINE

References checked by...   Initial rate... per... Date started... DEPT.

Entered on Payroll... Date... By...

Approved...

BCK CAT FORM 418

Exhibit III to Affidavit of James H. Mortimer.

125

INSTALLMENT NOTE — INTEREST EXTRA

$ 12ɔ.00   L.A.   California,   Jan. 19   , 19_63.

In installments as herein stated, for value received, ___I___ promise to pay to____
INTERNATIONAL SCHOOL OF BARTENDING _____ or order,

at _____

the sum of ONEHUNDRED TWENTYFIVE NO/00----_____DOLLARS

with interest from_____ on unpaid principal at the rate of

_____ per cent per annum, payable _____

_____; principal payable in installments of

_____ Dollars

or more on the_____ day of each _____ month, beginning

on the_____ day of _____

$125.00 Onehundred twentyfive no/00 dollars for six weeks Bartending
Course. Cash payment and there are absolutely no refunds.

_____

_____ and continuing until said principal and interest have been paid.

Should interest not be so paid it shall thereafter bear like interest as the principal. Should default be made in payment
of any installment of principal or interest when due the whole sum of principal and interest shall become immediately due at
the option of the holder of this note. Principal and interest payable in lawful money of the United States. If action be in-
stituted on this note.   I   promise to pay such sum as the Court may fix as attorney's fees.

Eric S. Galt

Tomás Reyes Ltd

NOTE — INSTALLMENT — INTEREST EXTRA — ATTORNEY'S FEES —WOLCOTTS FORM 1481   85179

Exhibit IV to Affidavit of James H. Mortimer.

126

RECORD OF PREVIOUS CONVICTION AND
SENTENCE OF JAMES EARL RAY, FOR ROBBERY,
IN ST. LOUIS, MISSOURI

IN THE CIRCUIT COURT OF THE CITY
OF ST. LOUIS, STATE OF MISSOURI
DIVISION NUMBER 12
Hon. John C. Casey, Presiding

1427-H 1959
THE STATE OF MISSOURI VS JAMES EARL RAY
On information for one (1) prior conviction of
a felony and robbery first degree
by means of a dangerous and deadly weapon.

Thursday, December 17, 1959

Now, on this day comes the Assistant Circuit Attorney for
the State, and the defendant herein, in person, in the
custody of the Sheriff of this City, and in the presence of
Richard Schreiber, attorney and counsel, in open Court;
and the jury aforesaid also come into open Court.

The jurors receive their given instructions from the
Court, and the argument of counsel is heard and concluded. Thereupon, the cause is submitted to the jury for a
verdict in the premises and they retire to consider thereof
in charge of a Deputy Sheriff, duly sworn according to
law, and said jurors having agreed upon a verdict are
conducted into Court by the Officer having them in charge
and in the presence of the said defendant, render the
following as their verdict, to-wit:

The State of Missouri vs James Earl Ray
On Information for Robbery First Degree by
Means of a Dangerous and Deadly Weapon.
"We, the jury in the above entitled cause, find the
defendant guilty of Robbery First Degree by
Means of a Dangerous and Deadly Weapon."
(s) William Wiley Gavin, Foreman

Whereupon, defendant, by his attorney, waives his
right to poll the jury, and said jurors are ordered
discharged by the Court from further consideration herein.

Whereupon, after the rendition of the aforesaid verdict
of the jury, and the acceptance of the same by the Court,
the Court now fixes and assesses the punishment of said
defendant at imprisonment in the Penitentiary of the State
of Missouri for the period of Twenty (20) years. Memo-
randum filed.

Friday, February 19, 1960

Now, on this day comes the Assistant Circuit Attorney
for the State and the defendant herein, in person, in the
custody of the Sheriff of this City, and in the presence of
Robert Schreiber, Attorney and Counsel, in open Court.
The Court orders the official court reporter to take notes
to preserve the evidence.

Whereupon, the defendant's motion for a new trial
heretofore filed herein is heard, argued and is by the Court
overruled.

Whereupon, said defendant is informed by the Court
that he has heretofore been found guilty by a jury of the
offense of Robbery First Degree by Means of a Dangerous
and Deadly Weapon, and being now asked by the Court if
he has any legal cause to show why judgment should not
be pronounced against him according to law, and still

failing to show such cause, it is therefor sentenced, ordered and adjudged by the Court that the said defendant, James Earl Ray, having been found guilty by a jury as aforesaid under an Information against him, be confined in the Department of Corrections of the State of Missouri, for a period of Twenty (20) years, and there be kept and confined until the judgment and sentence of this Court herein be complied with or until the said defendant shall be otherwise discharged by due course of law.

It is further considered, ordered and adjudged by the Court that the State have and recover of said defendant the costs of this cause expended, and that hereof execution issue therefor.

STATE OF MISSOURI
CITY OF ST. LOUIS

I, James H. McAteer, Clerk of the Circuit Court of the City of St. Louis, for Criminal Causes, which said Court is a Court of Record, having a Clerk and seal, certify that the above and foregoing is a full, true and complete copy of Verdict, Assessment of Punishment, Sentence and Judgment consisting of two (2) pages, one dated December 17, 1959 and the second dated February 19, 1960, in the cause of the State of Missouri, plaintiff, vs James Earl Ray, defendant, in cause No. 1427-H, as fully as the same appears of record and on file in my office.

Witness my hand and the seal of said Court hereto affixed, at office, in the City of St. Louis, this 9th day of June A.D. 1968.

[Signed] James H. McAteer
Clerk of the Circuit Court of the
City of St. Louis , for Criminal Causes

STATE OF MISSOURI
CITY OF ST. LOUIS

I, John C. Casey, Presiding Judge of the Circuit Court of the City of St. Louis, Division No. Twelve which said Court is a Court of Record, having a Clerk and seal, certify that James H. McAteer whose true and genuine signature appears to the foregoing certificates, is, and was at the time of signing same, the duly elected, commissioned, qualified and acting Clerk of said Court, and that full faith and credit are due to all his official acts as such, and that said certificate is in due form.

Witness my hand and seal hereto affixed, at City of St. Louis, this 9th day of June, 1968.

[Signed] John C. Casey
Presiding Judge, Cirucit Court of the
City of St. Louis, Division No. 12

STATE OF MISSOURI
DEPARTMENT OF STATE

To all to whom these presents shall come:

I, James C. Kirkpatrick, Secretary of State of the State of Missouri and Keeper of the Great Seal thereof, as custodian of the records hereinafter described, hereby certify that the official records of the State of Missouri show that John C. Casey is a duly qualified and appointed Judge of the State of Missouri, Circuit Number 22, and that his true and genuine signature is affixed to the attached record of the conviction and sentence of James Earl Ray.

In testimony whereof, I have hereunto set my hand and affix the seal of my office. Done at the City of Jefferson, this 10th day of June, A.D., Nineteen Hundred and Sixty-eight.

[Signed] James C. Kirkpatrick
Secretary of State

I, Warren E. Hearnes, Governor of the State of Missouri, hereby certify the foregoing attestation of records on file in the office of the Secretary of State of Missouri is in due form and has been made by the proper officer.

In testimony whereof, I hereunto set my hand and cause to be affixed the Great Seal of the State of Missouri. Done at the City of Jefferson, this 10th day of June, A.D., Nineteen Hundred and Sixty-eight.

[Signed] Warren E. Hearnes
Governor of the State of Missouri

UNITED STATES OF AMERICA
DEPARTMENT OF STATE

To all to whom these presents shall come, Greeting:

I certify that the document hereunto annexed is under the Seal of the State of Missouri.

In testimony whereof, I, Dean Rusk, Secretary of State, have hereunto caused the seal of the Department of State to be affixed and my name subscribed by the Authentication Officer of the said Department, at the city of Washington, in the District of Columbia, this eleventh day of June, 1968.

Dean Rusk, Secretary of State

By [Signed] Barbara Hartman
Authentication Officer, Department of State

131

THE LAW OF THE STATE OF MISSOURI
IN REGARD TO ARMED ROBBERY

I, James C. Kirkpatrick, hereby certify as follows:

1. I am the duly elected, qualified, and acting Secretary of State for the State of Missouri.

2. A part of my duties include being the keeper of the official statutes of the State of Missouri and the promulgation of same.

3. I hereby certify that Sections 560.120 and 560.135 of the Revised Statutes of Missouri 1959, define the crime of Armed Robbery First Degree by Means of a Dangerous and Deadly Weapon and delineate the limits of punishment of said crime. A true copy of said sections is set out hereinafter in full in words and figures as follows:

> Section 560.120. Robbery in first degree: "Every person who shall be convicted of feloniously taking the property of another from his person, or in his presence, and against his will, by violence to his person, or by putting him in fear of some immediate injury to his person; or who shall be convicted of feloniously taking the property of another from the person of his wife, servant, clerk or agent, in charge thereof, and against the will of such wife, servant, clerk or agent, by violence to the person of such wife, servant, clerk or agent, or by putting him or her in fear of some immediate injury to his or her person, shall be adjudged guilty of robbery in the first degree."

Section 560.135. Armed Robbery—punishment for robberies: "Every person convicted of robbery in the first degree by means of a dangerous and deadly weapon shall suffer death, or be punished by imprisonment in the penitentiary for not less than five years, and every person convicted of robbery in the first degree by any other means shall be punished by imprisonment in the penitentiary for not less than five years; every person convicted of robbery in the second degree shall be punished by imprisonment in the penitentiary not exceeding five nor less than three years; every person convicted of robbery in the third degree shall be punished by imprisonment in the penitentiary not exceeding five years."

[Signed] James C. Kirkpatrick
Secretary of State for the State of Missouri

I, Warren E. Hearnes, Governor of the State of Missouri, hereby certify that James C. Kirkpatrick, whose true and genuine signature appears to the foregoing certificate is, and was at the time of signing same, the duly elected, qualified, and acting Secretary of State for the State of Missouri, and that full faith and credit are due to all his official acts as such, and that said certificate is in due form.

[Signed] Warren E. Hearnes
Governor of the State of Missouri

AFFIDAVIT OF FRED T. WILKINSON

I, Fred T. Wilkinson, hereby state under oath as follows:

1. I am the duly qualified Director of the Missouri Department of Corrections.

2. All records concerned with the Missouri State Penitentiary are under my direct control and management.

3. Based upon records in my control one James Earl Ray, alias Eric Starvo Galt, W. C. Herron, James Walyon, John Willard, "Jim," was sentenced on February 19, 1960, of the crime of Robbery First Degree by Means of a Dangerous and Deadly Weapon and was received by the Department of Corrections on March 17, 1960, from which he escaped custody on April 23, 1967, leaving an unexpired term with legal expiration of March 16, 1980.

I hereby certify that the fingerprints and photographs of James Earl Ray attached to my Certificate of June 10, 1968, concerning said James Earl Ray, a copy of which Certificate is attached hereto, are original fingerprints and photographs of James Earl Ray taken from the files of the Missouri State Penitentiary.

Further affiant sayeth not.

[Signed] Fred T. Wilkinson
Director of Missouri Department of Corrections

Subscribed and sworn to before me this 12th day of June, 1968.

[Signed] Lorraine Oligschlaeger, Notary Public

DATE DUE